BRENT & CHRISTINE

TEACH KIDS TO

DREAM BIG

DREAMS?

Mike B.

Praise for Parenting with Dignity:

"I think one of the smartest things Mac Bledsoe talks about is raising your child without a fear of failure. My own parents functioned that same way with me and allowed me to become successful with what I do—writing and directing. I remember my Mom always used to say, 'Put on your magic boots. Don't let anyone tell you can't fly.' That stayed with me for a long time and is with me still. Mac is the same way—the way he has raised Drew and Adam; the way he talks about the topic of family. *Parenting with Dignity* helps parents in providing that environment where 'you are special,' where 'you can fly.'"

—Cameron Crowe, writer and director of *Jerry Maguire, Fast Times at Ridgemont High*, and other award-winning movies

"I think that Mac is on the cutting edge of what it takes to be a good parent. Mac can't put a band-aid on everything because there are going to be some serious problems with youth, but he talks common sense, he doesn't talk over anyone's head; he talks about real solutions for people."

—Peter King, correspondent for *Sports Illustrated* magazine

"*Parenting with Dignity* is an open, heartwarming, sensible approach for parents (and grandparents, too) who are raising their children. The delight in the book is the fact that Mac deals with real issues—the big decisions that your children will make when you are not around. The focus is that parenting should start early… but a parent can never be too late!"

—Alden Esping, Mac's YMCA leader and 1998 National High School Activities Director of the Year

"I found this book while Christmas shopping at our local Barnes and Noble bookstore. It was on a display table with other new releases. Both of my boys play football, and the cover caught my eye. I read the introduction and knew that I needed to have this book. I have not been disappointed by one single page!"

—Mother from Florida

"We are raising five boys and were excited to discover a program was in place that reaches out to parents like us! *Parenting with Dignity* guides, advises, and helps parents like us understand what it really takes to instill our values and morals in our children so that they can make good decisions. *Parenting With Dignity* can make a difference in one home and it can change an entire community."
—Jerry & Beth Blaze (Blake 11, Justin 10, Colby 8, Cooper 6, and Trevor 2) Cape Cod, Massachusetts

"In *Parenting With Dignity*, Mac untangles and demystifies the historical 'over analysis and frustration' associated with successful parenting. He does it so effectively a parent is no longer forced to wonder, 'how will I ever understand what I am reading and is it really possible to put this information to use?' This book is immediately useful the day you start reading it."
—Scott Driver, a married grandparent from Seattle, Washington

"Mac Bledsoe's book, if used with love, is the one parenting tool available today that is guaranteed to truly make a positive, life-long difference in the quality of a young persons experience on this Planet. Thank you, Mac, for sharing your life experiences, heart, and values in this wonderful guide for effective parenting."
—Father from Seattle

"Will this book ensure that your children will turn out to be the 'perfect' human beings we, as parents, wish them to be? No! No book could claim to do that. However, *Parenting with Dignity* will be the most effective tool in your parenting tool kit. Mac Bledsoe's personal values, and nearly life-long passion for assisting children, students, athletes, and parents, in being as 'successful' as possible in their lives are at the very core of this excellent parenting guide."
—Father from Maine

Parenting with Dignity

Parenting with Dignity

Mac Bledsoe

ALPHA

A member of Penguin Group (USA) Inc.

International Standard Book Number: 0-02-864425-5
Library of Congress Catalog Card Number: 2002113273

06   05   04   8   7   6   5   4   3   2

Interpretation of the printing code: The rightmost number of the first series of numbers is the year of the book's printing; the rightmost number of the second series of numbers is the number of the book's printing. For example, a printing code of 02-1 shows that the first printing occurred in 2002.

Printed in the United States of America

Publisher: *Marie Butler-Knight*
Product Manager: *Phil Kitchel*
Managing Editor: *Jennifer Chisholm*
Senior Acquisitions Editor: *Mike Sanders*
Development Editor: *Phil Kitchel*
Senior Production Editor: *Christy Wagner*
Copy Editor: *Nancy Wagner*

Cover Designer: *Doug Wilkins*
Book Designer: *Trina Wurst*
Creative Director: *Robin Lasek*
Indexer: *Angie Bess*
Layout/Proofreading: *Angela Calvert, Megan Douglass, Mary Hunt*

Contents at a Glance

Contents

Foreword

My Bledsoe family shares a common belief that the ills plaguing our nation and specifically our young people should be and can be cured at home by parents armed with effective parenting tools. Because I've seen firsthand the effectiveness of the commonsense parent-education curriculum my parents developed with their experience as public school teachers and as parents, I decided to throw the spotlight the NFL affords me into supporting this curriculum, Parenting with Dignity.

I feel blessed and fortunate to have been given some natural abilities that allow me to play football, a game I truly enjoy. I was further blessed with two wonderful parents and a family environment that provided me with strong basic values and a support system in which I could grow and develop and pursue my goals with their full support and unconditional love.

When I entered the NFL, I was often asked for money and time, and I was happy to contribute, especially when it would make the world a better place for kids. After three years, though, I decided I wanted to dedicate myself to something I believed in with all my heart. I believed my parents had some commonsense information that could give parents the tools to teach their children *how* to make good decisions. The outgrowth of these tools is that parents have a plan for how they will raise their children and what they will teach rather than parent in a "crisis-management" mode.

Parenting with Dignity is the curriculum developed by my parents, and it's based on two simple premises: (1) Your child will make *all* the big decisions on their own, and, therefore, (2) the way to ensure good decisions is to teach them how to make decisions based on your own family values and beliefs.

This book will teach you, as the parent, how to teach good decision-making. It is interesting for me to note that in 16 years of formal schooling I was taught not one thing about the most important job any of us will ever undertake: being an effective parent. Nowhere in school was I prepared for the most intimidating experience of my life: the 20-minute ride home from the hospital with my wife and our first son. Maura and I have made this trip more than once now. With the support of both our families, their strong basic values, their unconditional love, and the Parenting with Dignity principles, we are teaching our children how to make decisions, how to set and pursue goals, and how to grow into caring, responsible adults.

I invite and encourage you to learn and use the commonsense tools in this book to create a home filled with dignity, love, and children who know how to make good decisions.

With my sincere appreciation of your endeavor to be effective, dignified parents,

Drew Bledsoe

Introduction

Where did we get the title "Parenting with Dignity" for our parent-education curriculum? This explanation will give you an idea of the theme of this book, and will hopefully give you a guiding philosophy for raising your children.

In 1970, I was in the Army, running the personnel office at Fort Eutis, Virginia, and an amazing lady, Shirley Poe, worked for me as the office manager. She ran the office and set the tone for all of our business. Shirley's calm personality kept me sane despite the insanity of the Army, and she also taught me a ton. (She remains a friend today and is still teaching me.) One morning she was at her desk, greeting soldiers in her usual cheerful way, treating everyone with the same respect—rank never made any difference to Shirley. She had arrived at her usual time, 10 minutes early. About an hour into the morning, one of the privates who worked with her came to me and said, "Lt. Bledsoe, did you see what happened to Shirley last night?"

"No," I replied.

He dropped the newspaper on my desk and left. On the front page was a picture of Shirley's home. There was a 10-foot cross burning in her front yard. It was a time of great racial strife in our country, and the Ku Klux Klan was very active in the area because of the government-enforced school integration. The cross burning had to do with a marriage planned in Shirley's family that apparently didn't meet with the KKK's approval. Shirley is African American, and one of her relatives was marrying someone with lighter skin, or something equally ridiculous.

Simply put, Shirley had suffered a terrible and frightening indignity the night before. However, when I looked out my window and into the office, there she was, calm and cheerful as ever. I was dumbfounded by her manner after such a dehumanizing experience, so I called her into my office. Pointing at the paper on my desk I said, "I just learned about what happened at your house last night, and, Shirley, you have to help me, because I don't understand something. How can you be on time to work, cheerful, respectful, and kind to everyone after something so terrible has happened to you? How can you treat people so well when they treat you in such a disrespectful manner?"

She reached across my desk in that amazing and instructive manner of hers, patted my hand, and with her ever-present smile said, "Oh, Lt. Bledsoe, that's easy. In our family we are respectful and dignified not necessarily because the people around us are acting respectable or dignified: We act that way because we *are!*"

My life was changed forever! Shirley had just given me a standard for my life: In all situations, I get to choose how I deal with other people. Their actions do not dictate my response: I do.

Shirley Poe taught me to respond to all people with respect and dignity even if they were not respectful or dignified. She taught me that kids are people, too, and deserve our respect and dignity. Who are some everyday people who have taught you lessons about life? Have your children met them? Have you written down the lessons you learned from them for your children?

The Parenting with Dignity Program

When we began to develop this curriculum, I felt it was only fitting to title it Parenting with Dignity, because in our way of looking at it, parenting requires the same self-control. Your child may be acting rather undignified, lying there kicking and screaming in the entrance to the supermarket—but that doesn't mean *you* should lose your dignity! Parenting with Dignity focuses on the dignified approach parents must always take in working with their children.

The Parenting with Dignity program is, very simply, a parent-education organization. Parenting with Dignity is a resource for parents to learn new, essential parenting skills and gives them the tools necessary to create an encouraging and loving home for their children. Our existence is built around teaching the concepts presented in the course Parenting with Dignity as outlined on www.parentingwithdignity.com.

We contact parents through existing youth activities and agencies including Juvenile Court Services. We focus on these organizations rather than public schools, because schools are already overloaded with unrealistic expectations to "fix what's wrong with American youth." Many in our target audience would not bother to watch a prime-time TV program about effective parenting, so we partner with existing parenting-related organizations.

Our foundation has experienced a number of changes since its inception in May 1996. Yet the mission and the unshaken commitment to the children of America have not changed. My wife, Barbara, and I have spent much of our adult life sharing their vision of parenthood with countless groups of parents throughout the Pacific Northwest.

The Parenting with Dignity program offers three essential parenting-related products; our highly acclaimed video series, our newsletter, and our web-based resources. Now, as a direct result of the generosity and vision of our son Drew Bledsoe, the Parenting with Dignity curriculum is now available to anyone. The dream we share is that the Parenting with Dignity program will serve as an invaluable resource to all people who desire a world in which respect for others, and especially children, is a way of life.

I hope you will become part of making this dream a reality. Please consider becoming an agent for change—order a set of videotapes, hold parenting classes in your community, and donate to the foundation. Together we can change the world.

T-I-M-E

As I have traveled the nation for the past six years, I have been privileged to observe thousands of families and to interact with parents living in every imaginable situation. I began this journey with a belief that is even stronger today. I started off thinking that the biggest difficulty facing parents in modern America could be summed up in one simple word: T-I-M-E!

It was my belief that the primary reason parents have difficulty in their families is that *they simply are not spending enough TIME with their children.* I still hold that belief today and that belief is now supported by the previously mentioned parents. This book will be asking you to budget time for your kids into your day. If you are not willing to budget time to devote to your children, then most of this book will not be meaningful to you. You will hear this theme often in the course of reading this book. There is no switch for turning on "quality time"! There is time. Some of it may be quality time, and some of it may not be, but no parent has the ability to turn on quality time. All you can do is spend lots and lots of time with your kids. The more time you spend, the greater the chances that some of it will be true quality time that shapes the direction of your children's lives.

Having a Plan

A second observation I have made in my travels across America is that the biggest mistake parents make is approaching the task of raising kids without a plan; rather they crisis-manage, going from one crisis to the next. We hope this book becomes the basis for beginning to create a plan for raising your kids.

I won't pretend to say this book is all you need. As a matter of fact, this book should be viewed in just the opposite manner. In this book, I will try to focus on *how* you teach your children, not on *what* you should teach them. That is the portion of the plan you must create for yourself! I hope to give you a plan for raising your kids. I hope to offer you some skills for teaching what *you* believe to *your* children.

It Takes a Village to Raise a Child

One huge part of this plan can be expressed in the old, time-tested axiom, "It takes a village to raise a child." As you get to the latter parts of this book, I will propose to you that one of the most important actions you must take in raising your children to be happy and fulfilled adults will be to involve yourself with other parents in your community. Create the "village" that will raise all your children! Modern society has become fragmented and we need to act to pull the pieces together.

I will be proposing one sure way to build a strong village to effectively raise your kids: Form classes with the parents of the kids your children play and interact with. Discuss a common plan that all of you would like to use. *Parenting with Dignity* is designed to open the discussion between groups of parents. It is our hope that *Parenting with Dignity* will be a jumping-off place for a huge volunteer effort all across America for parents who are uniting to build hundreds of thousands of villages to raise millions of happy and well adjusted children.

It is so much easier to teach your kids to say "Please" and "Thank you" if every home they visit has the same standards. The same goes for appropriate dress, drug-free living, or any other standards the parents in your community select for raising your children.

I hope as you read through this book that you will always keep this question in the back of your mind: "How can I use this program for the benefit of my whole community?"

Together we can build a better world for kids, and we will build this better world one village at a time.

The Video Course

This is a course intended to be viewed by parents over a nine week period of time. The course consists of approximately nine hours of taped classes that are intended to be viewed by groups of parents one hour per week. Certainly viewing them individually works also, but we feel strongly that they bring the best results when viewed in small groups. Each tape is designed to be viewed in sequence, although each one is made so that if viewed alone it will give the viewer some immediately usable skills for working with children.

Also, included in the package is a Facilitator's tape which contains many suggestions for attracting class members, and setting up and conducting classes!

Order the videos by calling toll-free 1-800-811-7949; visiting our website, www.parentingwithdignity.com; or writing us at:

The Drew Bledsoe Foundation
730 Capistrano
Kalispell, MT 59901

This Book Is Dedicated to ...

My soul mate, my lover, my best friend, and my wife, Barbara.

Our two sons, Drew and Adam Bledsoe, who taught us more than all of the parenting books.

My parents, my roots and my wings, Stu and Betsy Bledsoe.

Barbara's parents, models of honoring commitments, Dick and Maxine Matthews.

The mentor who inspired the name of this book, Shirley Poe.

My role model, my teacher, the cowboy on our ranch, Buck Minor.

My YMCA leader who taught me that I was a participant in life and not a victim, Alden Esping.

A special thanks goes to all of my "professors," the students who graced my classroom for 29 years.

Chapter 1

A Simple Premise

Back in 1972, Barbara and I went through our most life-changing experience: the birth of our first son, Drew. Before I get into that earth-shaking experience, let me give you a little background about our family to set the stage. I had been in the Army, and we had been living in Virginia for two years. Barbara and I started dating in the eighth grade—and we are still soul mates, lovers, and best friends. We were married when I went into the Army, and the military experience had brought us even closer together, isolated as we were, away from family and friends. It looked like the end of my military service would finally bring stability to our lives, and we had decided to start a family. When I got out, we had been married four years and Barbara was six months pregnant with Drew, our first son.

We arrived back in our small hometown of Ellensburg, Washington, pregnant, broke, and unemployed. We did have the 10-foot-wide mobile home we had purchased while I was in the Army, but both of us were trained as teachers, and it was November. Teaching jobs don't open up in November, so I started searching the want ads and found a position as a remedial reading teacher in the nearby town of Kittitas.

Our next order of business was to visit the doctor and make arrangements for the upcoming birth. One "baby doctor" delivered two thirds of all the babies in town, so we went to see him for our first prenatal appointment. He was steeped in the medical opinions of the time and he viewed the birth process as a surgical event. This doctor talked about all kinds of medications and anesthetics and indicated almost immediately that he would not allow me in the delivery room: It was against hospital policy. Now, we weren't fanatics, but we had attended a childbirth class in Virginia (taught by a couple nuns—I'm not sure what they knew about childbirth), and it was important to both of us that I be there for the delivery. I don't think I would have made too big a stink about it before, but the nuns had convinced us that it was an important day in our lives and in the life of our child. I had been present for the conception, they said, so I should be there for the birth!

Well, we went out to our car after the appointment—and you fathers will know what I'm talking about when I say, "If Mama ain't happy, ain't nobody happy." I looked over and Barbara was crying, and I realized that we probably weren't going back to that doctor. Sitting there in the parking lot, I attempted to console my upset, pregnant wife, and we explored other options. I suggested looking in Yakima, where there were a couple hospitals and several medical offices, but the baby was due in the middle of February, and we can get some pretty harsh weather in that part of the country. Because Yakima was 37 miles away, along a winding road through a river canyon, we dismissed that idea. I wanted to be present, but I didn't want to be the *only* person present!

Finally I suggested we contact Dr. Jim Cobb to see if he would deliver our baby. Now, Jim Cobb was a sage, older gentleman, our family doctor and one of my dad's best friends. He practiced family medicine in a way that many doctors are going back to today. Almost every time any of us kids were sick (I have an older brother and two younger sisters), we saw Dr. Cobb in our own bedrooms right there on the ranch. He believed that people have minds, hearts, and souls, and often heal faster and better in their own home. As a matter of fact, he was the first man I ever heard say that if you want to stay healthy, stay away from hospitals!

I didn't even know if Dr. Cobb ever delivered babies, but we agreed that he was the type of man we would like to have attending such an important occasion. So we asked him. It was probably the best decision we ever made! His response was simple: "Oh, kids, I would be proud to do that!" So at about 10 P.M. on the night of February 13, when Barbara began labor, I called Dr. Cobb and he met us at the hospital. Immediately, a couple nurses loaded Barbara on a gurney and wheeled her into the delivery room. I was standing outside with Dr. Cobb and he was beginning to put on the green "pajamas" that doctors wear and I spoke up. "Sir," I said, "I haven't gotten an answer from you about whether I get to go in the delivery room with you … so I'm wondering, do I get to go?"

He weighed my request, then he grabbed another set of "pajamas" and threw them to me saying, "Put these on. I've always believed it's easier to get forgiveness than it is to get permission! Pull the cap down low and the mask up high, and maybe the nurses won't even know who you are. Let's go."

And now back to that life-changing moment ….

With Dr. Cobb's approval, I was in the delivery room and dressed for action. Two and a half hours later, our son was delivered without any complications. About 30 seconds after Dr. Cobb caught our son, cleaned him off, clipped the umbilical cord, and performed some tests, he handed this little person to Barbara and me, laying him on her chest. As he did so, he had big tears running down his cheeks. I think that explains why he was such a good doctor: The magic of human life could not pass him by without a piece of his heart going with it!

Only on Loan

Now hold onto your hats, folks, because we're at the critical part of this introduction to our curriculum.

As Dr. Cobb handed our son to us, he gave us the best piece of parenting advice I have ever heard, and his advice changed forever our view of our role as parents. *"Kids,"* he said, *"I want you two to remember something: This little fellow is not yours; he is just on loan to you for 18 years!"*

At that moment, we had no idea what Dr. Cobb meant. We certainly didn't know he had changed our lives with that sentence, but he had. Barbara was so preoccupied that she maintains to this day that he didn't say a thing! However, we went back two weeks later to see him for a check-up, and he rolled his chair over in front of us and placed a hand on each of our knees. (I think he wanted to make sure he made his point!) Then he repeated his statement: "Kids, just remember what I said in the delivery room a couple weeks ago. This little guy is not yours. He is just on loan to you for 18 years. If you can keep that picture in your head, it will serve you well in raising him."

We still didn't understand why Dr. Cobb was so adamant, but what he said next changed our lives forever. "Think of your child's life like a mortgage. Every day he will make a payment. By age nine, he will be a half owner of his life: By age nine, he had better be making half of his own big decisions!"

Now that was a truly foreign concept to Barbara and me. We had no picture of our child making half of his own big decisions by age nine. Especially not me—the way my dad had raised us seemed to be much more, "My way or the highway!" Looking back with some perspective now, I see that our dad was giving us lots of decisions to make all the time, it just didn't seem like it as I was living it.

"Mac and Barbara," said Dr. Cobb, "you both have a pretty clear picture of how much authority you'll have in the life of your child when he is two years old, don't you?"

I thought for a minute and replied, "Well, sir, we haven't thought that far ahead. We're kind of operating by crisis management. First a feeding, then a dirty diaper, then a nap, then another diaper, then another feeding, and so on, from one crisis to the next."

Dr. Cobb said, "Okay, I'm going to run through a list for you, and you tell me which things you feel you should be in control of when your son is two years old. Will you decide what time he gets up and what time he goes to bed?"

I replied, "Well, sir, our little guy is already in charge of the 'getting up' part. We're working on the 'going to bed' part, but we don't seem to be in much control of that either, right now. But by the time he's two, we hope to be able to have an established bedtime, yes."

He continued through a rather extensive list. "Will you be in charge of who he plays with?"

"Yes, of course, at age two, we'll pick his friends."

"Will you establish the boundaries of the play area?"

"Yes, we'll choose where he plays."

"Will you pick the books he reads?"

"Certainly," we replied, not seeing where this was going.

"Will you decide what he wears?'

"Yes."

"And will you decide what he watches on TV?"

"That's easy," we replied. "We don't have one!"

Now here's where Dr. Cobb shocked us. "Well, kids, I want you to remember the list of things you feel you should be in charge of when he is two. I want you to look at it often." Then shaking his finger at us, he said, *"Those are the things he should be in control of by the time he turns 16!"*

"You see, at age 16 he owns as much of his mortgage as you did when he was 2." Dr Cobb continued. "At age two, he only owns two-eighteenths of his life. You are still the majority owner at sixteen-eighteenths. But every day he makes another payment. By age 16, he owns the same majority of his mortgage that you owned when he was 2! He ought to decide what time he gets up and what time he goes to bed. He ought to decide what he eats and how big the portions are.

He should pick his own friends and choose what he does for recreation, and where. He ought to be picking the movies he watches and the books he reads." And on Dr. Cobb went, through the list!

Whoa! Now that was really a new idea to us! We had never thought of a child's life and education in that light before. I can't claim to know much of anything to be absolutely true, but let me tell you this: Dr. Cobb spoke the absolute truth that day. It remains the most profoundly accurate statement that I have ever heard about raising children.

You Won't Be There!

Whether you want to believe it or not, your kids will make *all* of the big decisions in their lives. Not some of, not many of, not most of, but *all* of the big decisions in their lives! Because when your child makes those big decisions, you will not be physically present!

At this point, I would like you to conjure up in your head the most realistic picture of your child that you can. Looking at that innocent young person, I want you to know with absolute certainty that that child will have to make a decision about whether to drink alcohol, smoke pot, or do cocaine, PCP, LSD, speed, or any other drug you want to name. You won't be there! The person offering the drug will not come over to your house and say, "Hi, Mr. or Mrs. So-and-so. Say, Johnny or Sally, would you like some crack cocaine?" The offer will take place somewhere when you are not around. And the scary part is, the one who offers drugs to your kids is not going to be some guy in a leather jacket from the bad part of town. The first "pusher" your kid will meet most likely will be one of the kids your child is playing with right now! It will be one of their friends, someone they grew up with.

It was at this point in a parenting class I was teaching in Selah, Washington, that a mother became very angry with me and stood up and announced, "I've had enough of this permissive crap. I'm leaving. But before I go, I want to tell you all why I am leaving. You don't know about me and you don't know about my family. I'm a reformed crack cocaine addict, and I am going to be there for my kids! I am not letting my kids make that decision!"

I replied, "Interesting concept, young lady. But before you leave, I would just like to ask you a couple questions. First of all, how old are your kids?"

"Nine and eleven," she blurted back even more angrily.

"And where are they right now?" I asked.

"Out on the playground with the other kids!"

"Oops, there you go," I replied.

"What do you mean by that?" she asked, even more angry than before.

"I thought you said you were going to be there for your kids. Tell me about school today. One of your kids must have flunked a grade and the other one must have skipped a grade, or they must have three grades in one classroom here in Selah."

Now she was really mad! "What are you talking about?"

"Well, you said you were going to be there for your kids when they make a decision about drugs. Obviously, you must have been with them all day today, right?"

"Of course not," she replied. "I'm a single mom, I have to work to support my kids."

"But you said you were going to be there for your kids when they make the decision about drugs. There was a big study on drug users and addicts in America a couple years ago that found that 84 percent of all drug addicts reported they got their first "fix" of drugs at school, from a friend, and they did not pay for it. There's an 84 percent chance your kids will make that decision at school, so if you're going to be there for your kids, you had better be with them every minute at school, too! But don't take my word for this, or the facts from some study: You're the self-proclaimed crack addict. You tell me, where did you get your first fix?"

"Oh, my gosh," she said as she thought back. "I was standing in front of my locker in middle school."

"And did you pay for it?"

"No," she mumbled quietly. "My best friend gave it to me."

Quietly I said, "See, your kids will make that decision out of sight of you."

Timidly, she sat down, ready to hear more.

It's important that I state, at this point, that I am not advocating *permissiveness*. I'm not saying parents should just let their kids do whatever they want to do. I'm just saying we cannot stick our heads in the sand and think that we can always guide and protect them. We cannot be at our children's side continuously to make the decisions for them.

Take sex as another example. Your kids will definitely make that decision, too. You could give each of your children a cell phone with your number on speed dial and I guarantee that you will *not* get a call asking, "Say Dad, ah, yeah, I'm parked out behind the high school and I could really use some advice ...."

Your children will make that decision also, and when they do, the only other person there will either be more confused or more enthusiastic than they are.

What about language? The words your kids will use in conversations will be words that *they* choose. Twenty-nine years as a public schoolteacher taught me that most parents wouldn't even recognize the language their kids use daily to express themselves to their classmates—and teachers!

Once I asked a mother to stop by my classroom after school. I had written six words on a piece of paper that I handed to her. I said, "These are six words your daughter used to express her displeasure with me for the grade she received on a paper she turned in yesterday."

After looking the list over, the mother was indignant. "My daughter would never use that one there, the one that begins with 'F'!"

"Please, let's not kid each other, ma'am," I replied. "I'm an English teacher, and she used that word four times in one sentence, as four different parts of speech, and each usage was grammatically correct! Now, please look at my face. I'm smiling, and I haven't come unglued. I'm just attempting to tell you that you had better teach your daughter that, even if she's mad and feels justified, her life won't go very well if she continues to express herself to authority figures with those words. If I had been her boss today, I probably would have fired her. If I had applied school rules, I would have suspended her. And if she had used those words to refer to some kids in this school, she might be recovering from a knife or gunshot wound right now!"

Your kids are going to make all of the big decisions in their lives. There's no getting around it!

Most parents I encounter in my travels around the country believe they can control their kids with artificial consequences—that is, punishment—that they apply after their kids misbehave. That tactic is absolutely worthless when it comes to the big decisions about drugs, sex, violence, and interpersonal relationships. Why? Because it is *failure-based*.

If parents wait until their child has tried drugs, is pregnant, has gotten a girl pregnant, or been severely injured in a fight, those parents will wish they had taught their child how to make good decisions *before* he or she was in the situation. Most of those decisions cannot be learned in the "school of hard knocks," because they cannot be made again or undone. A kid who tries cocaine will struggle with that drug for the rest of his or her life. A child who gets pregnant or fathers a child as a teen will live with that responsibility for the rest of his or her life. Abortion doesn't make it go away and neither does adoption. Some STDs, like herpes, are for life. We all know the terrible disease AIDS is incurable and fatal! Even angry words fired off in haste can alter lives as certainly as any disease.

Waiting until one of those decisions is poorly made and *then* trying to change it simply does not work! And what good is punishment then?

9

Parents who are deluded into thinking that they can protect their kids and will "be there for them" are in for a rude awakening: *They will* not *be there.* The kids will make those decisions away from their parents.

So what will kids use to make those big decisions? They'll use what they have been taught—unless, of course, they haven't been taught anything. If kids haven't been taught by parents to effectively make decisions, they'll use whatever they *have* heard or learned. They'll use whatever idea is in their head at the time. Many times they'll take input from whoever is shouting loudest at the moment.

At the time that drugs are offered, a child must have a clearly thought-out plan for the action to take *at that moment,* or the child will be in danger of making a bad, life-altering decision. The person offering drugs can often be very persuasive. "Oh, come on, everybody's doing it. Besides, who will it hurt? Just try a little bit. It'll make you feel great! Nobody will know. What's wrong with you? Are you chicken? Are you not cool?"

My experience over years of working with kids and parents tells me that the young lady in Selah is similar to many parents in America. Hopefully, her story can shock a few parents into realizing that their parenting techniques need to be reevaluated. Kids cannot be protected from making bad decisions with strict rules and artificial consequences. My work in prisons has taught me that. Most guys in prison don't even realize that their incarceration is a result of their own poor decisions, so how is that punishment effective?

Now, let's get back to what Dr. Cobb said in his office that day about the list of the things your child should have authority over by the time he is 16. He was telling us that we have the obligation as parents to teach our kids how to make decisions—good ones, and big ones! Dr. Cobb knew that our son would have to make those decisions for himself. He knew we would not be there to make those decisions for him.

Let me say it again: Our children will make *all* the big decisions in their lives. *We must teach them* how *to make them for themselves!*

Chapter 2

The Power of Ideas

Hopefully, I've established by now that your children will make all the big decisions in their lives. Not *some* of them, not *most* of them, but *all* of them! So now we get to the really meaningful part of this book: applying this fact to the wonderful job of raising kids. Here is the really critical question that all parents must answer:

How will kids make the big decisions in their lives?

And here is the simple answer:

The ideas in your head will rule your world!

The ideas in your children's heads will rule their world!

Your kids will make the big decisions in their lives with the ideas that are in their heads! They will use the ideas you have taught them ... unless you haven't taught them any. In that case they will use whatever idea they have found. Over and over, this statement must echo in your head:

"The ideas in my head will rule my world ... the ideas in my kids' heads will rule their world."

"The ideas in my head will rule my world ... the ideas in my kids' heads will rule their world."

"The ideas in my head will rule my world ... the ideas in my kids' heads will rule their world."

If you say to yourself, "My kids drive me crazy," you're right! Your kids will drive you crazy!

If you say to yourself, "I view my kids with a sense of humor," you're right! You'll laugh all the time with your kids, and their actions will bring you great joy!

If you say to yourself, "Oh, I hate these 'terrible twos,'" you're right! Your kid will drive you up the wall while he is two.

If you say to yourself, "Two-year-olds are in the most exciting time of child development, and I watch this growth with amazement," you're right! You will be amazed every day as you watch your two-year-old develop.

Once an idea gets into your head, it will rule your world. It doesn't matter whether the idea is right or wrong, good or bad, happy or sad, legal or illegal, moral or immoral, religious or sacrilegious. It doesn't matter where the idea came from. It can come from a book, television, or the pastor at church. It can come from something somebody did to you when you were a child, or from an experience you had as a child that you can't even remember. The idea can come from a song, or from guilt from a scolding long since forgotten. The idea can come from the Internet, a movie, or a poem that touches your heart.

The same is true for your children! The ideas in their heads will rule their world. If you are going to have success raising your kids, you have to get into the "idea business"! Parents must plant ideas in their children's heads that will allow them to make good decisions for themselves.

We must present ideas in behavioral terms that our kids can understand. We must present ideas *without anger,* in a manner in which kids can receive them, and we must accept that ideas often must be presented more than once before children can truly grasp *and use* the ideas in their decisions. We must understand that each child is unique and may require the same ideas presented in different ways.

Any attempt you make at influencing your children's behavior that does not *first* address what they think or feel about themselves is destined to fail!

Before we can understand how to shape those ideas, we first need to understand how ideas control human behavior. After all, kids are human, too!

What Ideas Will You Allow into Your Kid's Head?

"Judgment is a fine commodity, but it is virtually useless in the thick of battle!"

—George Washington

Simply put, what the great George Washington meant by this tidbit of wisdom is: *"We are going to fight with what is already in our plans, not what we think of during the fight!"* Applied to our situation as parents, we do what is already programmed into our heads. We will act upon the ideas that exist in our heads. If we have chosen our ideas well, we will make good decisions. If we have not made careful choices in advance, we will have to accept whatever actions the ideas in our heads dictate. "In the thick of battle" we act from training; we aren't able to come up with new and creative ideas during times of conflict. Your 2-year-old or your 16-year-old will follow the same process when confronted with a decision: They will make the decision based upon the ideas that they already have in their heads.

When a two-year-old decides to throw a fit in the grocery store, she's acting based on an idea about what has worked in the past. Yesterday, she wanted a cookie and started crying. Mom was on the phone, too busy to be bothered, and gave her the cookie. If crying got her a cookie, should we be surprised when later that night, she cries when she doesn't want to get ready for bed? What can you reasonably anticipate? The parent is tired and says, "Okay, if you stop crying, you can stay up for another 20 minutes." The child now has had *two* experiences in which she got her way by crying and kicking. Now she has an idea stored in her head. If crying has resulted in getting her way from Mommy or Daddy, it's only reasonable to expect her to try it again.

Now fast-forward to the grocery store. The child is in a situation where she wants something. It's not a conscious process. Just like George Washington said, she doesn't reason things out. She resorts to what has worked in the past, to the idea already in her head.

The Three Functions of the Brain

Let's look at this process in more detail—it's the foundation for techniques we'll be discussing in later chapters.

The Conscious Brain

The *conscious brain* is the part of your brain that does things you *think about*. Your conscious brain can only think about one thing at a time. The idea at the front of your mind at any given moment is your conscious brain at work. (If you want to hear it at work, just listen to your silent voice as you continually talk to yourself. That is your conscious brain.) If you can imagine that each of the three parts of your brain is a little person inside your head, the conscious brain is the *Actor/Actress* who plays your part in the world, always making sure you act just like yourself! It makes you dress like you, talk like you, walk like you, and do all the things you do. The Actor/Actress also becomes very uncomfortable if your actions do not match your script.

An example here will make this much clearer. Right now, hopefully, you are really thinking about this concept as you read. If someone came to you right now and interrupted you to ask where you left the car keys, you would think briefly and tell them where to look. If you couldn't remember, you might at least be able to name a few places where they might be. Either way, your thought process would involve your conscious brain. You stop, think, and come up with an answer.

14

Another example of your conscious brain at work would be reading a map in a strange city to find the best route. You may use some stored knowledge of where you are now and how to use a map, and then consciously apply that knowledge to find a reasonable route.

Your children might use their conscious brain to find a route through a new room in a very similar manner. They look around and use their senses to take in information about the room and then consciously make decisions as they go through the room.

Those are examples of pretty low-level actions we take with the conscious mind. We use past experience and knowledge (what I refer to as ideas), add new information, and make a decision. This process is identical to the way we make larger, more complex decisions about much more important issues, and our children are no different.

Take the decision about using drugs or the decision about engaging in sexual activity. Our kids recall previously learned information, take in new information, and, in both situations, they make a decision to participate or not. Both of those decisions would involve high-level use of the conscious mind.

The Subconscious Brain

The *subconscious brain* does all the thousands of things you *don't consciously think about*. Many of these are autonomic functions like breathing, blinking, and heartbeat, but the bulk of the activity controlled by the subconscious brain is *learned!* You learn how to do these actions, then do them without conscious thought, as naturally as your heart beats or you breathe and blink. Early in life you learned to tie your shoes and brush your teeth. Maybe it took a while, but today you can get up in the morning and brush your teeth while your conscious mind is thinking about your upcoming day. You get dressed and put on your shoes, performing some or all of that process with no conscious thought. You just do it from habit, just like breathing—you don't have to think about it.

Like the examples I used in describing the conscious brain, the preceding examples are pretty simple. However, many actions we perform every day are just as natural as breathing, blinking, tying our shoes, and brushing our teeth, but have far greater consequences. We store many ideas about ourselves in the subconscious part of our brain—ideas that have a great influence on the outcomes we experience. We learn how to interact with other people. If a child learns that whining gets adults to give in to demands, the child will often whine to get a variety of desired results. On the other hand, if a child learns that saying please results in more positive outcomes from his parents and other people, he'll use that behavior. In either case, once the effective behavior is learned, it will be used much like we tie shoes, with little conscious thought.

The subconscious brain is your *Scriptwriter,* who continually writes a script for your Actor/Actress (conscious brain) to follow in playing your part in the world. As you learn things about yourself, the Scriptwriter records them so you can act without having to think consciously about every action. Your script runs the gamut from things as simple as tying shoes, buttoning a shirt, or combing your hair to complex activities like driving a car, operating a word processor—or giving instructions to your kids! The subconscious brain also stores ideas you've learned about your traits and capabilities, such as, *I'm messy,* or *I'm not very good at sports and math,* or *I'm a happy person who finds the silver lining in every dark cloud!* It can even store information like, *I whine when I want something!*

All your Actor/Actress has to do to act like you in most situations is check the script. You go through life effortlessly and efficiently, doing most of what you do naturally because the Scriptwriter has learned how you act and written it all down in your script. However, although the script is often accurate about your abilities, it can just as easily be mistaken. Either way, the Actor/Actress has no choice but to follow the script—or be made very uncomfortable.

In fact, most of what is in the script comes not from the actual experience but from *self-talk.* It is not what happens to you that shapes your script as much as *what you say to yourself* about what happens to you. The key is to keep your focus on the positive aspects of what happens to you—such as what you learned from something negative—and repeat those aspects to yourself. (You'll learn much more about this important concept shortly ....)

The Creative Subconscious

The *creative subconscious* has the job of making the conscious and subconscious work in harmony with each other. Think of it as the part of your brain that keeps you sane by making sure your actions are consistent with your stored or learned script of how you should act. The creative subconscious is the *Director* of the movie of your life, making sure the movie matches the script. Who makes the Actor/Actress uncomfortable when they deviate from the script? The Director. To do this, the Director has been given a *Three-Part Contract*, which must be followed if the movie, a.k.a. your life, is to be properly produced.

The Director's Three-Part Contract

1. The Director Must Balance the Actor/Actress and the Script

The metaphorical contract states that the Director must make absolutely certain that the Actor/Actress's actions balance with the script written by the Scriptwriter. If your conduct isn't following the script, the Director must restore balance as quickly and as efficiently as is possible. The Director has control of all the psychological and physical reactions necessary to achieve this balance—even if it comes at great cost to you!

Let's say you're asked to do something out of character, like unexpectedly being asked to sing a difficult song in front of strangers. The Director will call up many common responses to this perceived imbalance between what you're being asked to do and what you would normally do—like giggling, fidgeting, appealing for help, sweating, getting red in the face, increasing your heart and breathing rate, becoming light-headed—even running away! If your script says singing is something you're neither good at nor comfortable with, then the Director has no choice but to make sure you fail—and not just fail, but also to make you very uncomfortable as you try.

Do any of these behaviors remind you of behaviors your kids exhibit when they are asked to do things they don't want to or are afraid to do? When you ask your child to clean up her room, does she ever become fidgety or begin some other activity? Or maybe she just asks for you to do it, or at least help, even though you know she is capable of doing it on her own. Her Director is making her Actress balance her actions with her script, which says "I don't clean!" You might recognize other scenarios, like asking your son, who has learned that he is shy, to walk up to a stranger and say, "Hello," or asking a daughter who has learned that she doesn't like vegetables to take a bite of salad.

This process becomes critical when the script begins to govern crucial behaviors in later life. You will learn much more about this in later chapters.

2. The Director Is Amoral

The Director does not make decisions about right or wrong, good or bad, happy or sad. The Director simply looks at the script and produces the movie as it is written. The Director doesn't evaluate talent or ability, or select what actions are best for you. The Director simply follows the script, directing the performance of the Actor/Actress so it matches the script as closely as possible.

This explains why some people who seem to have remarkable abilities never rise to their full potential, while others with seemingly insurmountable handicaps achieve astonishing things. At this point in explaining this concept in parenting seminars, I have asked thousands of people in audiences all across America to stand alone in front of the group and sing "The Star-Spangled Banner." I have had only one person actually accomplish the task—a choir director with a script that said he was a good singer. In every other case, the people either refused to sing or failed miserably. You see, in our society, a very common script says, "I can't sing!" With that as a script, it's not hard to understand why the people sing poorly or not at all. Their Director looks at the script and tells the Actor to fail!

I would like you to imagine a couple situations and then experience, on a very personal level, the interaction of your conscious, subconscious, and creative subconscious.

First, I would like you to imagine that you are at the funeral of a respected dignitary. Now imagine me walking up to you and informing you that in 5 minutes you will be asked to walk to the podium and speak for 10 minutes to this large audience of strangers and friends about your philosophy of life. Speaking in front of an audience is almost universally feared among Americans. It's pretty safe to assume that most anyone reading this book has a script in his subconscious brain that would say, "I hate to speak in front of audiences."

Now, look at what your Director, your creative subconscious, does as you consider the imbalance between your script and what your Actor is being asked to do. Your script says, "I am not good at this," so your Director begins trying to get you out of the situation, or at least makes you very uncomfortable.

Let's try another more graphic example. Let's say you come into a restaurant and are seated at a table that has been partially cleared. On the table is a plate with a serving of mashed potatoes and gravy. Imagine me asking you to pick up a fork and take a bite.

In our society, we've been pretty universally taught not to eat off used plates in restaurants—it's in the script! "I don't eat off used plates in restaurants! YUCK!" It might be possible for you to consciously deduce that the potatoes hadn't been touched, but it would still be very difficult to overcome the script that you learned long ago about not eating from used plates in restaurants. For many people, just imagining that little scenario can cause nausea and revulsion. The creative subconscious is very powerful in controlling human behavior!

19

We humans simply do not always do our best or do what is right. Rather, we act based upon the stored ideas in our heads—no matter what the idea is. *The ideas in our heads rule our world!* The solution we must always strive for is to create positive scripts in our heads—and, most important, *in our children's heads!*

3. The Director Cannot Change the Script

The metaphorical contract states that in maintaining or restoring balance, the Director does not have the ability or authority to change the script to match some new action by the Actor/Actress—even though the new action may be more to everyone's liking. Once the script is written, the movie must be produced to match!

Reality on the Set

Now, what we have described in this model could potentially produce a very depressing plot for your life or the lives of your children. If your script calls for poor performance, you—and your children—are doomed to that level of performance forever. The script may be wrong, but the Director will make the Actor/Actress follow it. Could you and your children be trapped in a bad movie?

The exciting solution is that your Actor/Actress *does* have access to your Scriptwriter—and thus to your script! Your conscious mind has the ability to rewrite your script through *self-talk*. The continuous conversation between your conscious and your subconscious brain is the process by which your mind programs itself and rules your actions. The key is to become *conscious* of what your *subconscious* brain is putting in your script—and if you don't like it, change it! In this way, you *can* consciously choose the ideas that rule your world.

This is important for two reasons as you develop techniques for working with your kids. First, you must use your own self-talk to structure your own behavior, or else you're doomed to repeat the parenting scripts you have in your head—and they may not all be the most positive. Second, you must encourage your children to develop their own productive self-talk to create positive scripts in their heads. The rest of this book will be dedicated to teaching you parents effective techniques to promote positive, productive behavior in yourselves and your children by changing both your scripts *and* your children's.

Taking Action

1. Write down three behaviors you have learned but no longer have to consciously think about to perform, like showering, tying your shoes, making your bed, or *I am so busy I can't seem to spend time with my kids.*

2. Write down three behaviors your children have *learned* but no longer have to consciously think about to perform. Try *not* to list negative or annoying behaviors. List things like dressing themselves, speaking to you, knowing their favorite food, or any special ability they may have.

3. Write down three ideas you have allowed to rule your world that are positive and produce desirable outcomes. Think of ideas such as *I'm very productive in the morning; I love talking to people;* or *I'm a good listener, and they like to talk to me; I'm very organized;* or *I'm very frugal and get the most out of my money.*

4. Write down three ideas you have allowed to rule your world that are negative, and perhaps not even accurate. These are ideas that you would rather *not* have ruling your world, such as *I hate Mondays; I can't relate to my kids; I'm always unlucky;* or *I never have time to do the things that are most important to me.*

5. Write down three ideas your children have allowed to rule their world that are positive and produce desirable outcomes, such as *I'm a happy kid and I never let things get me down; I love music and how it brightens my life; I'm extremely curious and constantly learning new stuff;* or *I love my relationship with my grandparents.*

6. Write down three ideas your children have allowed to rule their world that are negative, and perhaps not even accurate. These are ideas that both of you might rather not have ruling your child's world, such as *I often blame someone else for my mistakes; I'm not always*

friendly and respectful to my family and friends; I don't always give my best effort at school; I'm terrible at math; or *I'm a loser.*

Keep in mind that the purpose of these exercises is to maximize the positive and productive ideas in your mind and the minds of your children. We also hope you can identify and eliminate—or at least minimize—those negative, nonproductive ideas. Over time, you may find that those negative ideas have simply lost influence, as positive ideas displace those that don't produce the kind of behavior you—and your kids—want to demonstrate.

Chapter 3

Getting the Behavior You Want

It is imperative that parents establish expectations for children's behavior. There's no getting around it: Parents have the ultimate responsibility for teaching their children their family's moral, ethical, and spiritual standards for behavior. It all starts at home!

I'm aware that some people in our society will try to tell you that you have little or no influence over your children. I will tell you that the opposite is true. I believe that the only way that you, as a parent, will not be the most powerful influence on the ideas that rule the world of your children is if you choose to "abdicate the throne." If you give up trying to be a positive influence on your kids, then I agree that you will be replaced by people and influences you didn't—and wouldn't—choose.

To establish expectations for your children's behavior, you must first understand that you do not directly control your children's behavior. *They* control their behavior. All you can do is teach them the values that influence their own decision-making skills. You teach them how to make good decisions for themselves.

Kids are born with a will of their own. Anyone who doubts this has obviously never tried to put a two-week-old child to sleep when the child has decided to be awake! A parent who thinks they will always be able to control the behavior of their children is mistaken. I'm not saying parents shouldn't guide their children, and I'm *certainly* not saying that kids should be allowed to do anything they want. I'm saying that a parent must guide the child to make good decisions—on their own—because that is all parents can do! It all begins with establishing a solid relationship and a set of guidelines and rules for the child to use in making decisions.

Parents can set standards for behavior and delude themselves, through constant supervision and harsh punishments, into thinking that they are in control, only to find that the first time the child is outside their immediate supervision, he chooses to violate the rule! One of the most at-risk groups for binge drinking and abuse of alcohol on college campuses is the kids who were raised in abstinent homes, where they were forbidden ever to be around alcohol and monitored by tight curfews and constant parental supervision. What happens when these kids arrive on campus and the parents who kept them from drinking are at home? They're totally unprepared to make the decision alone. All they learned at home is to let someone else make their big decisions. All of a sudden, the loudest voice they hear is saying, "Come on—drink this!"

When parents teach their kids to make the right decisions for themselves, kids—on their own—go right on doing what they've always done: Making good decisions based on sound logic, morals, and values! The child with sound ideas to rule his world is the child best armed for taking on the world!

Good decisions require lots of accurate information, and lots of guidance in how to use the information to make decisions. Right now I want to help you, the parent, select your goals for guiding children's behavior.

There's only one kind of discipline: *self-discipline!*

What Kind of Wizard?

In *The Wizard of Oz*, Dorothy, the young girl, is whisked away to the Land of Oz by a cyclone and is told that the only way to get home is to go see the Wizard. Dorothy sets off to find him, and along the way she meets the Scarecrow, who wishes he had a brain; the Tin Man, who wishes he had a heart; and the Cowardly Lion, who wishes he had courage. They all decide to go along with Dorothy in hopes that the Wizard can help them, too.

They have quite an adventure in the Land of Oz and encounter all kinds of hardships and difficulties battling the Wicked Witch of the West. When things go wrong and they're sad, the Tin Man cries real tears. When they need intelligent solutions, the Scarecrow comes up with them. And finally, when they need courage, the Lion has developed a real roar, and he steps up to defend them all.

When they get back to the Wizard after their adventures, he is exposed as an imposter. What will they do? Where will they get what they thought only the Wizard could give them? The answer is simple. The Great and Powerful Oz is wise enough to show them that they already had those things! He gives the Tin Man a clock to be his heartbeat, gives the Scarecrow a diploma to show his intelligence, and gives the Lion a medal to prove his courage. The Wizard of Oz simply gives them symbols of powers they already had. (How he got Dorothy home is another story ...!)

Parents are very much like the Wizard. We cannot give our children any powers or abilities they don't already have. *What we do is enable them to recognize and use what they have.* If we give them solid ideas upon which to make decisions, they will amaze us. They'll make better decisions for themselves than we ever could. They understand their situation better than we do. They see things and have critical information that we do not. They have better input.

What kind of wizard do you wish to be in your children's lives? A positive one who challenges them to use all of their potential, or a negative one who places limits on them and their potential? Decide what you want for your children. Once you have a clear idea of what you want, your strategy for helping them use their own abilities to select the desired behavior often is obvious. Let's move on to an understanding of this simple concept.

Merely Demanding Obedience from Children Is Dangerous!

So often our method for shaping our children's behavior is to demand obedience. In most cases that's what was done to us when we were growing up. For a number of reasons, demanding obedience is a dangerous way to manipulate a child's actions. If you're not physically present at all times to ensure obedience—and we've already shown that you won't be—your efforts often can fail. We must not only decide *what* we want our kids to do, but also *why* we want them to do it!

"Back in *Your* Day?!"

To steer ourselves away from simply demanding obedience, we must focus on being able to logically explain to our kids why we are asking them to behave in a particular manner. We have to eliminate from our minds an idea that guides many of our decisions—often without our even being conscious of it—about how we'll raise our kids. This idea comes in the form of familiar phrases like, "Back when I was a kid ..." and "If I had done that when I was a kid, my dad would have ..." or "Back when we were in school they used to ..."

Sound familiar? As parents we must never allow ourselves to fall into the trap of saying "it's always been that way" or "that's the way my parents did it" to justify our actions, or explain them to our kids. It is imperative that we be able to give sound behavioral, moral, spiritual, ethical, or legal justifications for the behavior we are teaching to or demanding of our children. "Because that's how I was raised," is never a good enough reason to repeat a behavior with our children. You may do a lot of things with your kids that your parents did with you, but you better have a better explanation than that. Everybody's parents

26

make mistakes—you will, too!—and we're doomed to repeat them if we don't think long and hard about the justification for the actions we take with our kids.

Two historical examples demonstrate the obvious problems with doing what has always been done before. Slavery was a part of early American history. We certainly wouldn't advocate continuing that practice simply because it was done before. Neither would we teach our children that women should be second-class citizens, even though they weren't even legally recognized by the Constitution until the 19th Amendment was adopted early in the twentieth century. Saying that women shouldn't vote only because they never did in the past would be ludicrous.

Likewise, it would be foolish for us to tell our children to wear certain clothing simply because it was appropriate in the past. The same goes for hairstyles and many standards of behavior. Now, we're not proposing the abandonment of all standards of dress for young people. Rather, we're saying that we ought to make the standards logical and explainable, not just base them on blind obedience and statements like, "If I had dressed that way my dad would have killed me!" *Why* do we have dress codes? That's the critical question for kids.

When you can explain behavior logically to your children, they can understand for themselves and, because they understand, will *choose* to follow your guidelines, rather than simply *obey* you. Obedience teaches children to listen to an "outside voice" to determine their behavior. Because you won't be there when your children make their biggest decisions, it won't help them to do what you say, out of obedience. You want to make sure you've given them an *inner voice*—one that helps them reason out a good decision for themselves.

Teaching for Great Results

Two behaviors that are almost universal among Americans reveal some surprising facts about the effectiveness of some of our teaching techniques. In the last six years, I've conducted a little informal survey as

I have traveled across America, and it has yielded some interesting and thought-provoking data. I hope this information will stimulate some serious thought about the techniques we use in teaching life's important lessons to the next generation.

I've asked literally tens of thousands of Americans if they know how to ride a bicycle and found only two women and one man who can't! I've also asked that same large sample of Americans if they wrap presents and give them to loved ones at Christmas. Only 13 men and 7 women did not! (And it wasn't because they didn't know how, but because they had decided not to for moral or religious reasons.)

"So," you ask, "what's so amazing about that?" Simply this: Bike-riding and gift-wrapping at Christmas are both learned behaviors! It appears to me that, as a society, we do a masterful job of teaching those behaviors! Almost everyone in America knows how to ride a bike and wrap and give presents at Christmas. And yet, other more critical behaviors like honesty, integrity, teamwork, compassion, reliability, respect for private property, respect for diversity, diligence, love, manners, and many others are taught much less universally and much less effectively!

It occurred to me that it might be interesting to examine why our society is so successful at teaching bike-riding and gift-wrapping. I thought it would help me learn how to be more successful in teaching life's critical lessons.

How do we teach kids to ride bikes? They don't learn by reading a manual. They don't learn by listening to us talk about how to do it. And they sure don't learn by watching *us* do it! Kids learn to ride a bike when we put them on the seat and turn them loose! They learn by experience, and they want to learn because we paint such an exciting picture of how great it will be. What do we do when they tip over or fall down? We pick them up, dust them off, give them encouragement and instruction, and put them back on the seat to try again. We might give them training wheels or run along beside them to offer occasional assistance, but the learning comes because they are on the seat with the handlebars in their hands!

How well do you think kids would learn to ride bikes if, the first time they fell off, we ran to them, scolded them for falling off, told them how disappointed we were with their failure, took the bike away, sent them to their rooms, and grounded them for three weeks to think about how to ride a bike? Do you think that technique would produce a whole society that can ride a bike? I sincerely doubt it.

Why, then, do we think that we can teach responsibility to our children by scolding them when they fail, sending them to their room, grounding them, and taking away further chances to be responsible? Shouldn't we put them back on the seat? Should we not pick them up, dust them off, give them some encouragement and instruction in responsibility, and then, as soon as possible, give them another chance to be responsible? Shouldn't a child who has acted cruelly to another child be given instruction in kindness, encouragement that we believe in their kind nature, and then, immediately be given the freedom to be kind from now on? Lectures about how it was done in our day, and commands to be obedient would do little to change their behavior.

Now, let's take a quick look at gift-wrapping and exchanging at Christmas. Why are we so successful at teaching this rather complex and wonderful act of love, kindness, joy, and sharing? We succeed for many of the same reasons we succeed in teaching kids to ride bikes: We let kids learn by experience. Even before they're old enough to understand much about what's happening, we let them experience gifts by giving them some. We continue giving them gifts every year and, as soon as possible, we let them experience the thrill of *giving* by helping them to wrap gifts and give them to others. We also surround gift-giving with a huge pageant of excitement. We count down the days. Our whole society talks, with excitement and anticipation, about the magic of the Christmas spirit. And—*surprise*—they all end up gladly participating in giving and receiving gifts every year!

What if we, as a society, were to celebrate ethnic diversity with the same joy, ceremony, anticipation, and enthusiasm we assign to giving gifts at Christmas? Interesting to ponder what might happen in the next generation. We could demand it out of blind obedience, but I doubt we would get much compliance.

A simple adjustment in our society's priorities might bring about some amazing and welcome changes in the behavior of our youth. It might even bring some welcome changes in adult behavior! What behaviors would you like to see being taught universally in your community? We believe that we as parents, and as a society as a whole, can promote change if we choose to, but communities like yours all across this great land must commit to it.

Good Decisions Are Better Than Obedience!

Obedience doesn't teach children *how* to make decisions. Give them your guidelines in the crucial areas, then let them make their own decisions. If they make a mistake, pick them up, dust them off, give them some more guidance, and put them back on the bike.

Make the freedom to decide fit your personal standards of safety, morality, and good sense. Place boundaries around your children and let them decide within those boundaries. You will find that your children will use what you have taught them to establish far more strict boundaries and limits on their behavior than you would have.

When our boys got their driver's licenses, we didn't tell them what time to come home; we asked them what time they would be home. They always established earlier times to come home than we would have. Of course, we gave them lots of information to make the decision. First, we pointed out that there was almost nothing legal for minors to do after the hour of midnight. We also pointed out that more than 80 percent of the teen crime in America is committed between the hours of midnight and 3 A.M. Then I drove down to the police station with them to show them that at midnight on both Friday and Saturday, the police department put out two, three, or four extra prowl cars to go out and catch teens misbehaving.

Then we always had the kids tell us about some activity they would suggest to their friends after the game or the dance or whatever activity they were intending to attend. We always wanted our kids to be thinking beforehand of something to do, so they wouldn't wind up getting involved in something simply because they lacked a plan. It was amazing to watch them bring their friends over to work on a car stereo, play a game, or make a pizza. They always had a plan for entertainment that was fun, legal, and healthy. We didn't require them to come home—we helped them to make the decision for themselves.

Now, there *are* situations where parents should *not* let young children learn from mistakes. If the behavior is (1) illegal, (2) immoral, or (3) potentially harmful to themselves or others, a parent must act as the adult and intervene. Sometimes the risks are too great, the stakes too high to allow kids to learn from their mistakes. The best policy is to stay in the prevention mode and help them to make good decisions before the fact, so they don't get into those situations in the first place.

In any of those situations, it may be necessary to restrain the child from "falling off the bike" and harming themselves or others by their mistake. Don't make the mistake, however, of thinking that the restraint has taught them something. A boy who is hitting his brother might need to be sent to his room to prevent him from injuring the little guy, but going to his room doesn't teach him how to negotiate or be kind the next time.

Behavioral Motivators Kids Can Understand

Let's find some alternatives to obedience and discipline as a method of behavior control. By having more reasonable goals for behavior control, you'll kill two birds with one stone: Your children will be more self-directed *and* more self-reliant. They'll have reasonable limits on their behavior and they'll grow in their ability to make good decisions—even when they're out of your presence. So let's explore valid reasons other than "Because I said so!" to teach your children to make decisions to limit their behavior.

Respect for Authority

"Do it because it's the law." Teach your children that a civilized world will always have rules and laws. Teach them that rules are not an annoyance; they are an aid to us all. Rules and laws protect our rights, privileges, property, and safety. Explain to them that chaos would result from a society without stop signs, property laws, and rights to privacy, opportunity, expression, and freedom from injury. (Note that it is almost impossible to teach respect for laws and rules if your children see you violate those same rules and laws. You can't speed and then demand that your children drive the speed limit!)

This education about rules and laws can start at a very early age. It really works to point out to kids as young as four or five that a busy intersection simply would not be negotiable without traffic lights. I watch our son teach his kids the meaning of red, yellow, and green lights and how they protect all of us, and it's easy to see why, at three and four, they're able to negotiate intersections by looking at the lights and knowing how to decide when to stop and when to go.

As I work in juvenile prisons (and adult prisons, for that matter), it never ceases to amaze me how almost every kid who is in trouble with the law has little or no knowledge of the very law they have violated! A child who has a knowledge of laws and an ability to use that knowledge to make decisions is far better equipped for successful living than a child who doesn't!

Behaving Like Ladies and Gentlemen

"Do it because society says so, in ways that are less formal than laws." You won't be fined or sent to jail for violating these rules, but they can be just as important. Manners, customs, and social standards often dictate how your child's character is judged. Teach them that they can act any way they wish, but other people have a right to their own response—and people's responses are often predictable. "You can cut your hair in a Mohawk and dye it orange if you wish, but remember that many people will discount you as a meaningless person. It may not be right, but it shouldn't come as a surprise! The same goes for public conduct. Loud, rowdy behavior will be viewed as immature and disruptive and looked down upon."

Once I encountered a student of mine wearing his baseball cap at a funeral we were both attending. I leaned over to him and said, "Wearing a baseball cap here at this funeral will not get you sent to jail, but it will be judged as extremely rude and disrespectful by everyone here." With just a little instruction about an unwritten rule, he quickly complied. I doubt he would have made the same decision if I had just told him to get it off his head because I said so.

You won't face a judge for these infractions, but the court of public opinion can be equally harsh! Children need to know the reasoning behind many of those rules.

An interesting thing happened to me when I started to teach our sons about some of the unwritten rules of society. I discovered that some were pretty silly and I really needed to question them myself! I found some things that I was doing out of my own blind obedience that really weren't too wise. For example, I had always been taught to eat everything on my plate. I discovered that a much better standard for how much I should eat was to listen to my body. When it said I was full, it was healthy for me to listen despite what society had taught me.

You Need Their Help

"I can't do this without your help." Many times a simple request for help will work wonders on a child's behavior. Think about it: When you ask your kid for help, you're sending some very important—and complimentary—messages. First, you're saying, "You are a capable person, and I trust you to do this right." Then, you're saying, "I've come to you, of all the people I know, to ask for help." Finally, you are saying, "In a family, we *all* need each other!" Don't be surprised if your child starts to turn to you for help after you model that behavior for her/him.

A mother once told me she asked her daughter, who was reluctant to make her own bed, if she would help her make Mommy and Daddy's bed. She was shocked when the child gladly helped. She was even more amazed when, later the same day, the daughter asked her to come into her room and help her make her own bed!

When our sons were 9 and 15, we bought a computer. Barbara and I felt it was necessary for our kids to keep up with all the changes in school and in society. Let me tell you, it was a big step for our family! Barbara and I researched and shopped and found the best deal we could, but this was still a big investment for us.

I'll never forget the day we brought the whole thing home. It was in six or seven boxes. Into the room came Adam, our nine-year-old, with a kitchen knife to help us unpack it. "Stand back," I cried. "We paid more for this than we did our car! Let me do this."

Then I thought for a minute and asked myself, *"Who in this family knows how to set up a computer?"* The answer was simple: the boys. So I asked them to set it up.

In half an hour they called upstairs for me to come and look. I went down into the study room, and they not only had our new computer set up, they had all the manuals organized on the bookshelf and all the boxes stacked up neatly along the wall. Then I watched in amazement as they began to teach me all the things they could do on our new computer!

By my simply letting them help me, they had received some pretty important lessons:

1. I valued them.
2. They could do things their dad couldn't do.
3. In our family, we draw on everyone's strengths.
4. In our family, everybody participates.

If I had my life to live over again, I would ask the help of both of our sons in managing our family bank account. I now know that they would have done a much better job than I have over the years. I could have gotten some real help with one of my weaknesses, and I could have given them very meaningful participation in our family operation.

There are so many places in our homes where we can ask for of our children's help. We can ask them to plan trips. We can ask for them to plan meals and buy groceries within a budget. We can ask them to organize family calendars. And the payoff is that it makes our life simpler and easier! We discover that we really do need their help.

Keeping the Peace

"Doing this will make life more peaceful and pleasant." Sometimes things that seem very basic to us have to be explained in behavioral terms to our kids because they haven't had enough experience to know them or discover them for themselves. Make your home a peaceful place by practicing what you preach. When your child has a request or asks a favor, don't scowl and put it off—show them they matter by doing it cheerfully and as soon as you can. Then watch their behavior when you make polite requests, rather than angry demands, for help or compliance. Children learn far more from our actions than from our words, and friendliness and cooperation are contagious! "Do as I say, not as I do" seldom works.

I've done a lot of close work in juvenile court with kids who are in trouble with the law. One of the first things I try to teach them is that happy people meet more happy people, and cheerful people get more opportunities than grouchy people. I try to get these kids to *experience* what I'm teaching rather than just telling them. I give them an assignment to go home and, every night for a week, run the vacuum cleaner around the living room. I tell them to do it when one of the adults in the home is trying to watch TV. I have them use the vacuum cleaner because it's *loud*—anyone in the room will have to notice. I tell them that they don't have to do a real good job, but if they find something on the floor that doesn't belong there, pick it up and put it where it belongs. Then I tell them to go into the kitchen when an adult is in there and take out the garbage. "If anyone asks why you're doing either one of those tasks," I tell them, "just say, 'I'm just trying to help out!' Then, on the night before our next class, ask to do something that you normally don't get to do, like play video games for an extra half-hour, or stay up and watch an extra half-hour of TV, or order a pizza."

They come back and say things like, "That's so great—it works!" or "Man, I couldn't believe my mom, she not only let me stay up but she actually played with me!"

I simply repeat what I told them the week before: "Cheerful, helpful people get lots more opportunities and spend time around happier people!"

Kids really like living in a happier and more peaceful environment, but few know how to build one. Teach them.

Being Their Own Boss

"This job needs to be done—by you." One of the most marketable skills in the world today is the ability to see a job that needs doing, figure out a way to do it efficiently, and DO IT. Give your children this ability by giving them jobs to do (simple at first) and then getting out of their way. Let them do the whole job, start to finish, and let the satisfaction of completing it be the payoff. A simple statement from you like, "Nicely done. Doesn't it feel great to do things on your own?" allows it to be their own accomplishment. They'll feel your respect, and appreciate the freedom of doing things on their own without your checking up on them.

I'm a great believer in democracy at home. I believe that it teaches kids to participate in their world and to think for themselves. I would suggest that it would be a great idea for you to hold a family meeting to divide the labor of running the home. Start by listing the jobs that need doing. Many parents tell us they're surprised that their kids often include tasks that they themselves just ignored or did themselves because it didn't occur to them that these were jobs the kids could share.

Then hold a "job draft" where everyone takes turns selecting jobs. Some parents have told us that when they do this with young kids, it works best if the parents choose two jobs to every one that the kids pick. The fact that the kids have some choice in the matter makes the jobs much more palatable than if they're arbitrarily assigned by the parents.

Once the draft is completed, everyone has his job to do, and failure to complete a job must be brought before the "family court." (Yes, you could get too carried away with this, but figure out what works best in the dynamics of your family.)

Some families have even told us that they let the kids bargain with each other and swap jobs to suit their own personal schedules and so on. Parents are included also. "Hey, I'll do the dishes for you twice if you'll put the garbage out for me on Wednesday morning."

Calling Their Own Shots

"You have a choice to make; what are you going to do?" This should begin as early as possible, starting with decisions like: "Which pair of socks do you want to wear?" Then start giving them bigger and bigger decisions to handle, like, "Here's the map. Which route do you think we should take?" Next time ask, "You know our schedule. What time should we leave?" Continually ask their opinion on issues in your lives. We learn to make decisions by making them. When they make a bad decision, don't punish them. Like I said earlier, "Put them back on the bike!" Tell them that you respect them for making the decision in the first place, then ask, "What did you learn from that decision? What are you going to do next? How do you think that will work?"

Listen and you will hear them ask the questions for themselves. Resist the urge to tell them your answers. In Chapter 9, you'll learn some great listening skills. Put them to work and just listen actively. When kids ask you things like, "Mom, Billy invited me to his birthday party and I told him I would go. Now Bobby has invited me to see that movie I've really been wanting to see. What should I do?"

Answer with another question that leads your child to make a decision; something like, "Gosh, that is a tough decision. How would you feel if it was your party and someone told you they were coming and then backed out to go to the movies? Let me know what you decide, because I know you will do the right thing."

Help your children make decisions before they are in tough situations by asking things like, "Well, this is your first time to go to the store by yourself. How are you going to act?" or "The fair is an exciting place. What will you do if some of your friends get carried away and start to behave in a rude or rowdy manner that you know isn't right?"

Keep giving kids lots of decisions to make and lots of feedback on how you evaluate their decisions.

Discovering the Joy of Learning

"Life is one big lesson." When learning is the goal, no action, mistake, or "behavioral adjustment" is ever a waste of time. When your goal is learning, mistakes are often the best teacher!

Remember, very little is ever learned when anger is involved, either on your part or on the kid's part. Buck Minor, the cowboy on our ranch, always used to say, "When you teach an animal a lesson through anger and meanness, don't be surprised if the meanness and anger are learned better than the lesson." When learning is the goal, anger has no role. If you or the child are angry, it is probably best to wait until the anger has passed to attempt the learning.

Often, taking the time to teach is the longest and most difficult way to change your child's behavior, but it winds up being the best way because it results in lasting behavior change. If you're driving the car and the kids are quarreling in the backseat, it may be quicker and easier to separate them than it is to teach them negotiating and compromising skills. However, in the long run, separating them winds up teaching the opposite behavior from what you probably want. Separating them teaches them that when people disagree, the best course of action is for them to be separated. (No wonder we have such high divorce rates!) It would be much more logical to teach two fighting kids some effective ways to deal with quarrels and disagreements that will serve them for a lifetime. It takes planning, thought, time, patience, and *love* to keep learning as the goal.

It may take longer to bring about behavior changes in a four-year-old. However, if you take the time to teach *skills*, rather than mere obedience, when they're four, then when they're fifteen you'll no longer have to make them obey, because what you taught them at age four will still be working. *Your child learned it!*

A mother came early to one of our parenting classes and said she had a problem with her nine-year-old son and wanted my help. "He just won't sit still in church," she said.

"So tell me the rest of the problem," I said.

"That's pretty much it, he just won't sit still in church!"

"Wow," I replied. "If I were your son, you'd be having some real trouble with me, too. I'm not very good at sitting still." Then I went on, "Do you have anything else you want him to do in church?"

"What do you mean?" the mother asked, confused.

"Well, do you want your son to listen to the scripture readings and gain some ideas he can use to guide his life?"

"Well, yes, of course I do," she replied.

"Then I suggest you find out what is going to be read in church and read it at home a few times before you go. You might discuss the scripture reading on the way to school, or use it as the basis of a discussion about a television show you watched together. Many times the Bible can be difficult to understand and a little discussion before hearing the scriptures read in church might help him take it in. Do you want your son to learn anything from the minister's sermon?"

"Of course I do!"

"Well, find out the topic before going to church and then discuss the topic around the dinner table on Wednesday night. Find an article on a similar topic for your son to read sometime in the week before going to church on Sunday.

"Do you want your son to know that when people sing together with a common belief that something really powerful happens?" I asked.

"Why, yes," she replied. "I think the singing is one of the most important parts of the church service!"

"Have you ever listened to kids sing 'Rudolph the Red-Nosed Reindeer' at school?" I asked.

"Yes, they really sing out. I wish our son would sing in church like he does at school."

"There's nothing harder to do than to sing a song when you don't know the words or the melody! He sings out at school because he knows the song. Get a hymnal from church and practice singing the songs to be sung at home a few times! I know how powerful and comforting it is to sing familiar songs with a message. 'The Old Rugged Cross' was sung at the graveside during my father-in-law's funeral and I sang along because it was a song that I knew from my childhood. The song quieted me and comforted me."

About six weeks later I saw that same mom. "How's it going with the sitting still in church?" I asked.

"Gosh, I haven't even thought about him sitting still!" came the reply. "But my son takes notes during the sermon now that we discuss the topics. As a matter of fact, last Sunday he cornered the pastor after church because he had some suggestions for him the next time he spoke on the topic of honesty!"

Reassess and Reapproach

Remember, you can never assume a child has learned anything until she uses it in the appropriate context to bring about positive change for herself. By that I mean, don't assume your children have learned anything until they use it in their lives! Also, saying something is not the same as *teaching it*. So often we hear parents say, "I told him. I don't know what's wrong, but he's not doing it!" Well, you may have said it, but it doesn't sound like he learned it. You haven't taught a concept until the child's behavior changes. You, as the parent, are responsible for your child's learning, and a change in behavior is the only measure of success in teaching.

If the behavior hasn't changed, you may have to keep trying, or try a completely new method. Keep the anger out, and don't give up! You may not succeed on the first few tries, but *you haven't failed until you stop trying.* Too many parents say, "I've tried everything," and give up, instead of saying, "Oops, that's another teaching method that doesn't work in this situation—I'd better keep looking for another way!"

My wife, Barbara, was having a really difficult time with our sons leaving wet towels on the bedroom floor every morning after their shower and leaving their dirty underwear on the bathroom floor. Every morning it was the same drill: Go in the bathroom, drop your shorts, take a shower, get out a new towel, dry off, wrap it around your waist, go to your room, drop the towel on the floor, and get dressed for school.

She had asked them a thousand times to pick up their underwear and hang up the towels in the bathroom where they would dry rather leaving them in a heap on the floor to get mildewed. But the routine didn't change. The towels would build up on the bedroom floors until she could no longer stand it and she would pick them up and wash them. It wasn't working.

So she reassessed and tried another teaching tactic. She got two nice big red towels for Adam and two nice big blue towels for Drew. Then she explained one very simple rule: You may only use your own towels. The rest are off-limits. No exceptions.

First day, new regime: no change. Undershorts on the bathroom floor, colored towels on the bedroom floors. Second day, still no change. Barbara didn't say a word. Third day, into the bathroom like always, undershorts on the floor, jump in the shower. Then there was a change. There were no towels in the bathroom! Each boy had to try to modestly run back to his own room to retrieve one of his own towels. Yuck, those towels were wet—and they didn't smell very good!

It was interesting to watch Barbara realize that her previous technique wasn't working and, instead of getting angry, she changed her tactics—and got immediate results. She let the boys learn from their experience. It worked! Everyone learned.

It was also interesting to watch her try a different tactic with the undershorts on the bathroom floor. She carried about eight pairs of underwear from the bathroom floor out to breakfast one morning. "Can either of you young men tell me who should pick up these off the bathroom floor? When you tell me who should do it, I want you to tell me *why* that person should do it."

There was a long pause. "I guess we should pick up our own," they both replied.

"Okay, I'm here to help you to get this job done. How can we change things so you'll actually do what you agree you should do?"

"Why don't we get a clothes hamper for the bathroom?" one of them suggested.

That was all it took. In the end, Barbara didn't demand obedience, and she achieved a lifetime change in behavior.

Turning Obedience into Cooperation

Once you show your children the considerations we've discussed here for guiding their behavior—the law, social conventions, keeping things peaceful and happy—you seldom have to ask for obedience. They'll do what you ask because they've got their own very good reasons for staying in line. Then, when you *do* ask for obedience, it will carry that much more weight. You can save it for those times when obedience is *absolutely necessary*, like when the kid is running for the street and a truck is coming. When you cry "STOP!" you want to be darn sure they'll listen and obey—not ignore you because you've been shouting "STOP!" at them all day!

One more thought about obedience. Obedience between equal individuals is really what we call *cooperation,* and it's much easier to ask for if it is mutual. You'll get *obedience* at those critical times if your children can ask for your *cooperation*—and get it—when they need it.

We discovered that when we gave our kids the right to ask for our cooperation, they never abused it and in fact used it very effectively. One of our sons would use it when he simply did not feel like having a long or involved discussion. All he had to say was, "I'd rather not discuss this right now." We honored his requests and found that when we did discuss things, he was much more attentive.

Sometimes kids need to get our cooperation when we make unreasonable demands without realizing it. One time we were at a family reunion when one of our sons was thrown together with some cousins who were really teasing him. He finally needed our cooperation: "We have to leave now," he said, very forcefully. "I will tell you why later," he said, "but we need to leave now." After we left, he told us that he had tried everything he knew to avoid a fight, but a fight was about to happen, and he knew that wasn't right at a family picnic. He used his ability to get obedience from us to avoid a difficult and unpleasant situation.

Taking Action

1. Ask yourself the following questions: What is it that I want my kids to do? *What is my goal in asking for this particular behavior? Do I want them to respect authority? Do I want them to learn to make decisions? Do I want to have more peace around the house? Do I want them to demonstrate more appropriate or productive behavior? Do I need their help?* Write down a detailed description of your goal in asking for this adjustment of behavior.

2. Now it's time for some very careful thinking. Devise a strategy for accomplishing your goal. You may have to use one or more of the Five Rules you learn in the next chapter. You may also have to dream up a completely new strategy! Think about what you want. Think about your child, what she's like, and what's likely to get your message across. You may even want to think up a Plan B and a Plan C, in case Plan A doesn't get results.

3. Keep a daily record of your actions, your child's actions, and any observations that you have as you follow your plan for a week. Remember to record both positive and negative results.

Keep in mind that the purpose of these exercises is to maximize the positive and productive ideas in your mind and the minds of your children. In order to do this, you must actually try to structure effective thoughts in your own head as you plan strategies. Then, you must observe the resulting behavior in your children. Remember that unless your child chooses to tell you what ideas are in his head, the only way you have of knowing what ideas are stored in his head is by observing his behavior; so pay close attention.

A big part of this process involves not only creating positive change but also observing strategies that didn't work and devising new and better ones that will. Don't hesitate to list things that didn't work! Sometimes our best teacher is a mistake. A mistake only counts as a failure if you let it be the last time you try.

Also, when you try something that doesn't work remember the important phrase: "Keep the anger out!" Anger rarely results in productive thought processes or effective action.

Chapter 4

Five Rules for Parents

Avoid Crisis Management

Since Barbara and I began teaching, we've tried to identify some simple principles that are particularly effective in teaching kids the ideas that will rule their worlds. Over the first eight years of our teaching careers, we developed five rules. We then used those rules daily over the ensuing 21 years, so we have considerable experience using these principles in real life. At school we called them Five Rules for Teachers, and when we began working with parents, we called them Five Rules for Parents. We're really all in the same business!

We don't feel that there's anything magic or sacred about these rules—we've simply found that they work very well for us. You have our complete permission to scrap some or even all of them! However, if you do, we simply challenge you to create or restate a new rule of your own to replace any rule you discard.

Traveling the country for the past five years, I've come to believe even more firmly in these five simple rules. The more parents I meet, the clearer it becomes that the biggest mistake parents make in raising their children is that they are trying to do it *without any plan*. What I most often see is parents using *crisis management* as a plan! They may be using effective techniques, but they're waiting until there is a problem before they put the techniques to work. Their actions don't follow a plan, so their actions are often too late!

Most of the techniques we propose here are intended to be used *before* there is a problem. We recommend that parents teach the desired behaviors before the undesired behavior actually shows up. If parents wait until the child has hit his sister to teach him how to get along, it's too late. If parents wait until the kids are running wild in the grocery store to teach them appropriate public behavior, it's too late. Parents who wait until their daughter (or their son's girlfriend) is pregnant to teach appropriate dating behavior are too late. And tragically, parents who wait until a child has begun to experiment with drugs to teach them the advantages of drug-free living are usually too late.

Here's an analogy that might make this point clear. Imagine that I have just given you a nice new laptop computer—and you have no idea how to operate a computer. Now, I could set up that computer in front of you and then stand there with a ruler and rap your knuckles every time you touched a wrong key, but I doubt you would learn how to operate a computer very fast or very well. And if you sat there for a month, I seriously doubt you would discover on your own that pushing the "Ctrl" key and the "P" key simultaneously would cause the computer to operate the printer—and there's no *way* you would figure out that pushing "Ctrl," "Alt," and "Del" simultaneously would cancel a program that was jamming your computer! Wouldn't it be much easier for me to simply explain how to operate a computer before you started?

Most of the things we would like to teach our children are considerably more complex than pushing a couple keys on a keyboard, but I meet too many parents who are guiding their kids with the crisis-management technique of letting their kids try things, waiting for them to goof up, and then punishing them for their mistakes! It makes so much more sense to give the kids the guidance in the first place, before there is a mistake or a crisis.

The techniques we offer are intended to be part of a *plan of action* that parents follow long before problems crop up. This is a plan of *proaction* rather than a plan of *reaction*.

Let's take a quick look at these five rules to introduce how they work, then I'll discuss each one in detail in its own chapter.

1. Tell Your Kids What You Want Them to *Do!*

Tell your kids what you expect of them. End any criticism with a positive statement about the behavior you expect. This probably sounds too simple to mention. Well, let me tell you this rule exposes one of the biggest traps you will encounter in working with kids. I know because I was caught in the trap for almost eight years of teaching kids, both at school and with our own children at home. If you don't continually focus on consciously telling kids what you want them *to do*, you can get caught spending all your time telling them what *not* to do! The more kids you have and the more active they are, the greater the likelihood of getting caught in this trap of ineffectiveness. You have to state the expected or desired behavior in behavioral terms that your kids can understand.

You learned in Chapter 3 about the importance of explaining the reasons you expect certain behavior to your children. Once you have in mind a specific idea of what you want your children to do, the way to communicate that behavior will become very obvious. But remember, just because you have said something does not mean your children have heard it, understood it, and can translate what you said into productive action. Always keep in mind that it helps to include a "sales pitch"—a way of explaining to your child that the behavior *you* desire will bring about positive and rewarding outcomes for *her*. (Chapter 5 will be devoted to teaching Rule 1 in much more detail.)

2. Criticize the Performance, Not the Person

Criticism is often necessary in working on changing behavior, but it must remain just that: a criticism of the undesirable behavior, not of the child. As a matter of fact, it's usually possible to give your child a compliment while the behavior is being corrected. This sounds easy, but it takes great care and planning to do it. Plan ahead.

It usually works best if rather than saying, "You're so *whiney!* Stop whining about getting a Popsicle!" you can say something like, "You're usually such a happy kid that it surprises me that you would let a little thing like not getting a Popsicle bother you." Believe me, I know how easy it is, when you're trying to stop some undesirable behavior, to get caught simply describing that behavior. Statements like "You're always leaving your video games in the middle of the room," "You never clean your room," or "You just never speak to me in a pleasant voice" are really easy to make, especially if you have active, energetic kids!

Like I said, as a parent, you have to plan ahead so that you end up giving your kids something with which to build their positive script of their capabilities. (Chapter 6 will be devoted to teaching Rule 2.)

3. Don't Assume They Learned It: *Repeat It!*

Repetition is fundamental to all learning. Rarely do we ever learn anything on a first exposure, and our children are no different. When you set out to teach your child something, accept the fact that you will probably have to repeat it a couple times. Don't let this make you impatient, and don't let it make you angry. *Keep the anger out!*

Also, remember that if you have repeated something a number of times and your kids are still not getting it, then you need to find another way to say it. I've heard 50,000 parents say something like, "If I've told my son once, I've told him a thousand times!"

Well, there may be a slow learner in that house—but it is not the child! There are many ways to "say" something—and finding other ways to say it may help you further understand what *you* want. (Chapter 7 will be devoted to teaching Rule 3.)

4. What They Say to Themselves Is What Counts

Self-motivation is the only motivation that keeps working when you are not with your kids. No matter how much you would like to motivate and control your children, the controlling force in their lives will be what they tell themselves. If you were sitting in one of my workshops listening to me talk, what I said wouldn't matter if in your head you were thinking, "He doesn't know what he's talking about." You'd go home and forget everything I tried to teach you!

The techniques we use with our children must always be aimed at guiding them to phrase positive statements to themselves, to make the behavior you expect from them become the behavior they expect from themselves. How do you do this? By being someone whose behavior they want to copy and whose approval they want to receive. This teaches your children the fundamentals of value clarification and goal setting. (Chapter 8 will be devoted to teaching Rule 4.)

5. Send a Constant Message of LOVE

All humans learn to speak the language they are exposed to—and that is key, because love is a language! If we wish to have our children speak the language of love, then we must expose them to it continuously. There are two important corollaries to teaching the language of love to our kids:

- **Love is not just something you say, it is also something you do.** You can fake that you care, but you can't fake being there. To send a message of love to your children, you must show up. Love is not a spectator sport.

- **The time they most need to hear it may be the time you feel least able to say it.** When you are at the point of sending your children out to live in the street, that is probably when their hearts are most open to receive your message.

Now you've been introduced to the Five Rules for Parents. The next five chapters are devoted to discussing each of the five rules in detail.

Taking Action

1. Identify one behavior in each of your children that you would like them to exhibit. This may be something the child does that you wish to replace with a different behavior, or it might be something new you would like to see your child adopt. Describe the desired behavior in detail. (If you're attempting to *eliminate* a particular behavior, describe it in detail also.)

2. Read through the list of Five Rules for Parents and pick the rule or rules that you feel will work best to help you develop the behavior you selected in #1.

3. Describe the specific strategy that you intend to use each day to apply the rule you've chosen to encourage your chosen behavior in your child.

4. Keep a daily record of your actions, your child's actions, and any observations that you have as you go through this process for a week. Remember to record both positive and negative actions, reactions, and observations.

You must work to structure effective thoughts and strategies in your own mind, communicate them to your children, observe the resulting behavior, and modify your communication techniques as necessary.

It takes years for us to reach an adult level of sophistication and consciously control the ideas that rule our world. Your child isn't likely to understand yet, much less tell you, all the ideas that are in his head.

The only way you can know is by observing his behavior—so pay close attention. A big part of the process of creating positive change involves observing and analyzing your strategies, determining what didn't work, and devising new and better ones. Don't hesitate to list things that didn't work! Sometimes our best lessons come from mistakes. The only time a mistake counts as a failure is if you let it be the last time you try.

Finally, when you try something that doesn't work, remember two important phrases: (1) "That didn't work" and (2) keep the anger out! Anger rarely results in productive thought processes or effective action.

Chapter 5

Rule One: Tell Your Kids What You Want Them to *Do!*

As I said in Chapter 4, it may seem like an oversimplification to say, "You need to tell your kids what you want them to *do!*" But I know from experience that the more children you have and the more active and "headstrong" they are, the more this rule is needed. Without it you will be caught in a repetitive cycle of telling them "Stop this! Don't do that!" I know because, as I said, I was caught in this trap for the first eight years of my teaching career, and I struggled with it at home, too.

Dr. Bledsoe Gets Taken to School

I don't have an official Ph.D., but I do have one. My professors have been the students who sat in my classroom and educated me in the University of the Real World. Along the way I had two boys in particular who were two of my best professors. They taught me a great deal one year. Read carefully, and maybe you won't have to repeat my mistake!

Over the years, I had large classes with my share of strong-willed and active kids. Today, many of them would be labeled ADD or ADHD but nonetheless, they were in my room, and

I found myself spending most of my time reprimanding students for inappropriate behaviors that interfered with my ability to teach. Man, I was spending all of my time telling them what *not* to do!

Then, on my first day of teaching in the beautiful little town of Waterville, Washington, I had a life- and career-changing experience with two students. The day before the kids came to school, during our teachers' workday, one of the veteran teachers at Waterville High School pulled me aside and warned me about a couple of boys who would be in my first-period junior history class. The well-meaning teacher told me these two boys, let's call them Billy and Danny, were a two-man class wrecking-crew and that I had better be prepared for them.

This veteran advisor told me to lay down the law for Billy and Danny and get control immediately or they would repeat what they had done in many classes during their previous years in the Waterville School District, and destroy my educational atmosphere for the entire year. I wasn't about to let that happen! I took her advice and made out a seating chart for first period—and separated Billy and Danny by assigning them seats on opposite sides of the room.

Well, that was my first mistake. You see, these two young men were going to talk to each other during class, and seats on opposite sides of the room weren't going to decrease their chatter, only increase their volume!

After assigning seats, I opened the class the same way I always did: I handed out my Classroom Rules—three typed pages of them! You see, Barbara and I had begun our teaching careers as substitute teachers in the Seattle Public School system and as a substitute teacher I had noticed that almost every classroom had a set of rules. I began to copy these rules to use when I finally had my own classroom, and by the end of my subbing career I had a fairly sizable set. Then I went into the U.S. Army for two years, and they had a ton of rules. I didn't copy too many of the Army's rules because they didn't seem to apply to civilian life! Then I added a few rules I picked up playing football, being a member of 4-H and Cub Scouts, and so on. By this time, I had a pretty comprehensive list of rules!

Back to Waterville High. I began to hand out copies of my three pages of Classroom Rules. You might think this no big deal, but handing out pages like this can take up quite a bit of time. In a classroom of 27 high school juniors, there can be a whole bunch of behavior to correct if you decide you're going to correct it all yourself! I wasn't just handing out the rules, I was trying to establish that I was in control. I started on the right side of the classroom and counted out five copies for the kids in that row. Then, I had to stop and tell a boy on the other side of the room to stop talking, scowling at him in my most intimidating manner.

As I counted out the sets of rules for the next row, I had to reprimand a young girl who had begun to giggle. "Stop that giggling right this minute, or you and I will have trouble in this class!" Before I could finish counting, she began to giggle again. "This is now the second time I've had to tell you to stop giggling! Now, you get control of yourself, young lady, or you'll find yourself out in the hall and staying after school!" Again I began to count, but was interrupted by one of the boys in the back of the class who began to whisper. I slowly walked back there, and my size and scowl seemed to be sufficient to shut him up. Back to counting. By this time Danny, who was in the third seat in row one, had gotten his set of Bledsoe's Classroom Rules and had enough time to read over the first page, and here came one of the first lessons in my Ph.D.

Danny shouted across the room to Billy. If I hadn't separated these two, I might have missed the lesson, but I was able to hear Danny loud and clear: "Hey, Billy, have you got your 'Rules' yet?"

"Nah," Billy shouted back. "It's taking this bozo forever to hand them out!"

"Well, wait till you get one! These are cool! Look at number three! It'll drive Mrs. Johnson nuts next period. And then look at number seven—I would have never thought of that! Wow there's another page—no, *two* more pages! Man, these are cool!"

There in front of the class, I had a revelation. I had two boys in this class who were on a "Mission from God" *to disrupt my classroom*—and I had just given them a how-to manual. These two students were into pushing teachers' buttons, and I had just identified every one of my buttons! In my moment of panic, I couldn't decide whether to hand out the rules to the rest of the class, or collect all the ones I had already distributed.

I finished handing them out, but what I did at home that night changed the way I dealt with kids forever. Barbara and I decided to take a big black marker to our set of classroom rules and cross out every rule that told kids what *not to do*. I'm embarrassed to write this—but when we were done, we didn't have a single rule left! We had been spending all our time telling kids what not to do—never telling them *what the desired behavior was*! We were shocked!

So we decided to build a whole new set of rules that explained, in *behavioral* terms, just exactly what we *did* want our students to do. We could only come up with two new rules. As a matter of fact, we taught for the next eight years with only two classroom rules! (Mind you—I'm talking about classroom rules, not the "five rules for teachers.") Then after eight years my best friend, John Matau, who was the best school-teacher I've ever known, convinced us that we needed a third, so we added his rule to our list. We finished our teaching careers with three rules.

You're probably wondering what those rules were.

Rule 1: "When I talk, you listen."

Rule 2: "When I say get to work, you get to work."

And John's Rule 3: "Be respectful."

I received the second course in my Ph.D. the next day when I went into class and gave the new rules to my students. You see, you have to communicate expectations to kids in *behavioral terms they understand*.

Don't panic—this doesn't mean you have to start talking in the current teen slang you hear from the neighborhood kids. It simply means that you have to *define* the terms you use and not assume they understand concepts like "respectful" just because they have heard them again and again.

I realized almost immediately that I needed to define the personal pronoun "I" in our new Classroom Rule 1. "Class," I said, "I used a pronoun in that rule because it can mean any one of us in this room— and if I do a good job teaching this class, at least 75 percent of the time, the person speaking will be one of you! But we are going to listen to whoever is speaking. Each of you must defend to your death every- one else's right to speak, so that when it's your turn to speak, you can command the same degree of attention." (Here, the kids were getting a real lesson on how democracy is intended to work, as well as direction in what to do in this classroom.)

Then I realized that I needed to define the word *listen*. It seemed pretty straightforward to me, but I learned very quickly that it wasn't clear to my students. (Remember, the best way to communicate some- thing to a child is with methods other than words.) So I explained *listen* like this: "If you came to me and asked me if I wanted to go to the movies and my answer was a long pause, a look at my watch, a shrug of my shoulders, a look of disgust on my face, and a real quiet, 'Yeah,' what did I just tell you?"

"You just told us that you really didn't want to go!"

"No, I didn't. I said, 'Yeah.' Didn't you hear?"

"But you didn't act like you wanted to go!"

"That's right! You see, kids, you often listen more with your eyes than you do with your ears. Words do not convey all the meaning when someone speaks, and if you're not looking at them and their body language, you may get the wrong message. So in this class, when someone is speaking we are going to look at them! I'll bet one of the things that annoys you the most about your parents, teachers, or many adults is that when you talk to them they always seem to be reading the paper or looking at the mail or cooking, or doing something else and they never stop and look at you as you talk. We will not do that to each other in this class. When one person is talking, we are all going to give that person our complete attention and we are going to look at them while they are speaking."

All of a sudden, I was communicating exactly what the desired behavior was, and I was communicating it in behavioral terms they could understand. Man, it really blew me away when the students in my class began to listen! They finally knew what I meant—and maybe more importantly, they knew *why* I had made that rule.

With your own kids, you must be very careful to always explain exactly what it is that you would like them *to do*. As you explain it to them, always give them a "sales pitch" for this behavior and why you want them to use it at this time and place. That precise explanation helps them to make their own decision to comply, which is a lot different from asking for blind obedience. They are learning how to make the choice to obey, because they know how you made the decision in the first place. They are practicing the skill that truly will protect them in the outside word: good decision-making.

Classroom Rule 2 for our students, "When I say get to work, get to work," needed considerable explanation also. I told them, "Unless I appoint one of you to act in my place, the personal pronoun 'I' in this rule means me, the teacher. In this classroom of juniors in Waterville High School, the subject is U.S. history—and we are going to get to work on history!" I told them we were going to start every period with our notebooks open to our day-planners to keep track of the work we were going to do. I didn't threaten them with artificial consequences for not having their notebooks open on their desks. There was no first chance, second chance, third chance—I simply told them what was expected of them when the bell rang.

The response from my students the next day amazed me! They all had their notebooks open to their day planners. When I tell this story now to teachers and parents, someone in the audience always wants to know what I would have done if they hadn't done as I said. I answer them with a question: "Why do we always prepare for failure rather than success?"

After that lesson from Billy and Danny, what I always did was go to the desk of any student who chose not to have a notebook open to his or her day-planner and say, "I see you don't have a notebook, so I'll offer you a choice. Please borrow this notebook of mine for today, or you can leave this class. Look at my face so you get the whole message. I'm saying please, I'm smiling and being pleasant, but I mean this. I will still smile and say 'hi' to you in the hall, and I will still introduce you to my wife at the grocery store, but if you do not have a notebook with a day-planner on your desk, you cannot stay. What's your choice?" In 21 years, I had only one student choose to leave!

Teachers always ask, "Where did you get all the notebooks for the kids who didn't bring one or forgot it regularly?"

"Have you ever been in a high school on the day school is out?" I'll ask—knowing for sure that they have. "The halls are full of notebooks! I just pick them up and put them in my closet. I put day-planners in them and I've got more than I need for the next year!"

With your kids, always offer the choice of acting in the manner you have described. Most of the time, if I had a problem it was because I had not communicated the desired behavior in a manner they understood, or my "sales pitch" failed to convince them that the desired behavior would bring about positive consequences for them.

Giving Guidance—Getting Results!

We must program kids for success by guiding them in making good choices for themselves! Telling them what *not* to do is worthless to a child. (It's also worthless to say what *not* to do to an employee, a spouse, an employer, or an elderly parent—but this is a book about communicating with kids.) By showing them what you want up-front, rather than correcting misbehavior, you're showing them that you believe they have the ability to learn, and can be trusted to do the right thing when the time comes. When you *do* explain your expectations, you may be pleasantly surprised to find that they really can be trusted to make good decisions!

Telling children not do something or giving them negative consequences for doing the wrong thing is very much like the example I used earlier of my giving you a new computer—but no manual or personal instructions—and then sitting with a ruler and slapping the back of your hand every time you push a wrong key. Wouldn't you have a better chance of success if I first gave you the instruction manual and some guidance before I expected you to run it? We must do the same for our kids. Life is not an intuitive experience. The rules of society are complex, and we must teach our children how to act in any situation they may be in before they actually get there!

Kids will seldom self-discover politely removing their caps during a funeral if someone does not teach them. Most people won't self-discover society's appropriate dating and courting behavior if someone doesn't teach them. All too often, we leave these lessons of propriety to be taught by peers, by MTV, or the movies.

Here are a couple practical applications of this rule that might arise in your home.

Bedtime

First, let's deal with a common problem with many children: bedtime. Parents are tired at the end of the day and can be easily frustrated with children who balk and throw fits at bedtime. How can we avoid the nightly battle?

To start off with, let me simply say that you will be too late if you wait until the kids are in the situation and behaving in the undesirable manner. Explain the desired behavior for bedtime earlier in the day. Tell them exactly what you want to have happen at bedtime. "At 7, Mommy and Daddy will set the timer for 15 minutes. When the timer goes off, it's bedtime!" Take the child over to the clock and show them when 7 is coming. Then show them how the timer works. Set it and let your kids experience 15 minutes, so they have some idea of what it means to have 15 minutes to do things of their choosing before going to bed.

Lay out their pajamas and let them know exactly what will happen when the timer goes off announcing bedtime. "When the timer rings, we'll go into your bedroom and change into your pajamas, then we'll go into the bathroom and brush your teeth. When your teeth are brushed, we'll go back into your bedroom, you'll jump up into bed, and then I'll sit down with you and read two of your favorite books. Let's pick the books right now and lay them out so they'll be waiting for us tonight!

"When we're finished reading, you will lay down in your bed, put your head on your pillow, and go to sleep."

Then, about 20 minutes before it really is bedtime, remind your child of your earlier discussion. It might go something like this, "Sally, it will be bedtime in about 20 minutes, and I want you to remember what we discussed this morning. Your pajamas are all laid out. When the timer rings, we'll change into your pajamas and then go into the bathroom and brush your teeth. Then you'll go into your bedroom and jump into bed, and I'll sit down with you and read a couple of your favorite books. Are the books that you picked out still by your bed?"

When we suggest this plan to many parents, they immediately want to argue and tell us it will never work. Granted, it may sound pretty simple, but it really *does* work! It's amazing how dramatically you increase the chances of getting kids to do as you say if you teach them exactly what you want them to do well before the event. By talking about bedtime when it's still hours away, you've removed the threatening aspect. You're describing the desired behavior *before* they have an emotional reaction to the situation. They know it's not bedtime, so they're more at ease and able to listen to what you want. Bedtime will not come as a surprise, and here's the key: By doing this, you'll get them to *agree* to the desired behavior. When bedtime comes, they may still be reluctant to go, but they know they've already agreed to it. It's not just an order from you: You discussed it together! The *decision* to go to bed without a fuss will start coming from *inside* them! It may take a few repetitions, but after a couple days of telling kids exactly what you expect of them in a given situation, you'll usually end up with positive results. You must model "calm" and "quiet" if that is what you want from them.

As your kids get older, it might be a good idea to actually include them in the process of establishing their bedtime. Obviously, you're not going to have a teenager set out pajamas and select books you'll read to them, but a discussion of how many hours of sleep they need to be rested and healthy are an essential part of the process of establishing a bedtime. Beginning with the time that your child must get out of bed in order to get to school on time and then counting backward the required sleep time will establish a reasonable bedtime.

The skill of time management is easy for a child to master, but it requires guidance and instruction. Without guidance, most teens will try to make the decision based only on what they want to do in the evening and fail to factor in necessary sleep time and time for morning preparations. I also know many well-guided kids who use the process daily—and I know many adults who have yet to master it!

(Of course, if this rule always worked, we wouldn't have had to devise others! Don't give up if you find a situation where you don't get the desired results with Rule 1. We'll give you additional rules for other situations.)

Shopping for Success

Let's tackle another situation difficult for many parents: taking youngsters to the grocery store. First of all, let's face it: When we take children to any store, we're competing with the best minds in marketing, and they have created an environment aimed at seducing even the most resistant adults into impulsive purchases. These people save their most powerfully enticing displays to tempt our children. We know we will find toys and candy on lower shelves where kids will see them. We know the stores will put sugary cereals in colorful displays with cartoon characters and superheroes. The checkout counters will be surrounded with toys, candy, and gum. We're up against a pretty powerful opponent!

What are we to do? We know we have to anticipate a difficult situation any time we take our kids to the grocery store or the mall. However, that anticipation—and preparation—arms us. It's almost pointless to tell kids in advance that they're not going to get a toy or any candy. That is like me telling you, "Don't kick elephants!" When I give you that command, what happens in your mind? You picture kicking an elephant! My telling you not to kick elephants has created a picture in your mind of exactly what I do not want you to do.

Have you ever warned a child not to spill her milk—and that's the very next thing that happens? This might explain why: By telling them to not do it, you may have placed the idea in their mind that keyed their action.

If you prepare your kids for a trip to the grocery store by telling them all of the things *not* to do, you may in fact be increasing the chances of them doing them!

We have to create a plan with our kids about what they *are* going to do!

The best strategy for teaching kids to handle themselves in a grocery store is to give them a plan that focuses on going in and getting what you've agreed upon. Make out the grocery list together at home, and give each child tasks to do in the grocery store: Put one in charge of pushing the grocery cart, and give each one a list of items to find and put in the cart. Have them learn how the store is laid out so they know where to find the items on their list. If you are going to split up to find things, establish where you'll meet. By giving them responsibilities, you compliment them with high expectations. Get them involved in making it a successful shopping trip.

Of course, you're not denying them candy just to be mean. Candy and toys cost money, and they aren't part of your food budget! When kids get old enough to understand this, give them a certain amount of money to purchase the items assigned to them. Anytime they purchase their assigned items for less than you budgeted, let them keep the saved money to either spend at the end of the shopping trip or, even better, add to money they're saving for larger purchases. Teach your kids how to shop for bargains and best buys.

Let them see that by going to the store with a plan, the family sticks to its budget and has money to do other things. Start out with $50, and show them that by carefully planning there will be $18 left to go out to dinner or get a movie on the way home. Nothing teaches like real experience!

The Hard Stuff

Now, let's try dealing with a more complex and dangerous behavior parents confront when their kids are a little older: facing the decision about the use of drugs and alcohol. Telling your kids, "Just say no! Don't do drugs!" is worthless! You must tell them exactly what *to* do!

Following you will find specific wordings your child can use as you help him learn what to say to another kid who is offering him some drug. I would strongly suggest that you not only say these to your child but also write them down and give them to your child. Also, I would strongly recommend that you role-play this with your child three or four times. In some situations, you play the part of the kid offering drugs to your child. Other times, you can play the part of your child and have them play the dealer. In the latter scenario, pay close attention: You may learn some valuable information about situations your child anticipates or may have experienced already.

While role-playing, try to trip up your kids by challenging every response they give—just like a teenager might do. Have them practice sticking to their planned responses.

1. **Name the illegal activity.** "Do you know that possessing marijuana is a crime called 'Minor in Possession of a Controlled Substance'? And did you know that the amount you have in that baggie constitutes a felony?"

2. **Describe the consequences of the illegal activity.** "Do you know what a felony is? That's a crime for which the penalty is over a year in the state prison with the hardened criminals. You won't just go to juvenile detention or the county jail—and in this county many juveniles are being tried as adults. Did you know that if you are convicted of a felony you can be denied access to one third of the jobs in America? You cannot be a fireman, policeman, schoolteacher, or work in the airline industry. You cannot serve in the military or work in any job requiring a security clearance."

3. **Suggest an alternative activity.** "Why don't you get rid of that stuff and let's take the pickup truck over to my place, put a blue tarp in the bed, hook the garden hose to the hot water faucet in our laundry room, and fill my pickup bed with hot water. Then we'll drive it across the street to the church parking lot and have the only portable hot tub in town! We can call up some other kids to come and join us. I already checked with Pastor Smith and he said it would be okay!"

   Or "Let's tack some paper plates on trees in the woods outside of town and write numbers on them and we can play Forest Golf! You play the whole course with one club. Start at a given spot and tee off toward the tree marked with a #1 on it. You count strokes just like regular golf, but instead of putting the ball in a hole you must have your ball within a club's length of the tree."

   Teach your kids to always have at least three alternative activities in their head to suggest in place of messing around with drugs.

4. **Remove yourself from the situation.** "Hey, if you guys are going to do this, I'll just go home. Stop the car and let me out there at that phone booth. When you decide to do something else, give me a call, but if you're doing something illegal, I can't hang out with you."

5. **Always have an out.** We have a "secret word" in our family. I told my sons that if they were ever in a tough situation and needed out, just to call me and act like they were ordering pizza. "Place the order and in the process of the order just say our 'secret word.' Obviously, you have to give the address when ordering a pizza. Hang up, and I will come and take you out of the situation." My gosh, I don't care if I'm popular—I'm the English teacher and football coach at the high

school, so I'll never be popular with the teenage crowd! I could get them out of the situation and save face for them.

Let's say your son is at a party and he discovers some kids in the basement smoking pot. He's uncomfortable going in the room and taking a stand against the behavior, but knows that he needs to get out of the situation.

All he needs to do is to dial your number and order the pizza mentioned earlier. You drive over and angrily demand to see your son. When he comes out, you start yelling at him (for the benefit of anyone listening). You tell him to get in the car—you're taking him home to mow the lawn with a flashlight because he didn't do it during the day like you asked. Once in the car, congratulate your son for getting himself out of a difficult situation.

In another possible situation, your daughter is at a slumber party and some of the kids are talking about sneaking out to go to the home of a boy whose parents are gone. Your daughter doesn't want to go, but she's afraid to say so for the usual teenage reasons. Because she has just practiced this with you before she left, she knows exactly what to do. She tells everyone that she promised to call home to check on the status of her grandmother in California, who had surgery today.

When she calls you, she says, "Hey, Mom, I'm calling like I promised. How's Grandma doing?" That's your clue to tell her you have some "bad news"—and that you'll be over to pick her up right away. When you pick her up, in front of the other girls you simply tell her you'll give her the details on the way home, and the two of you leave quickly.

Just like the preceding situation, you congratulate her for getting herself out of a difficult situation. Telling these "white lies" is something you can talk about as a family if you need to, but the risk of children having no way out is tremendous.

As always, I welcome and invite you to try and suggest other strategies that work! The key is to develop strategies and teach them to your children *before* they're in a difficult or dangerous situation.

Once you describe for your children exactly what to do in a tempting situation, be sure to practice again with them before they get ready to go out. Make sure they repeat for you the two or three suggestions they have for an alternative activity. The more clearly they have the ideas formed in their head, the greater the possibility that they'll use them to make a good decision.

Where Good Decisions Start

You see, by giving your kids a clear idea of what to do in a tough situation before they're actually in it, you give them a starting point for making their own good decisions. The best protection you can give your kids is a wealth of positive ideas to use in the face of tough decisions. As we have said before and as you will hear again before you finish this book, the ideas in the heads of your children will rule their world. Your obligation to your children is to give them a library of positive ideas to use in tough situations.

It's really not much different from my telling you that if you want to print something on your computer, you push Ctrl+P. Telling your child what to do at bedtime, or what to do at the grocery store, or what to do when confronted by friends doing drugs is just about as simple!

Recently, our son Drew and his wife began the process of moving into a new home. They purchased a beautiful, 30-acre home in a quiet rural setting. On their property is a very scenic two- or three-acre pond. As we were visiting the property, a family friend observed that she had scary visions of Drew and Maura's three sons and the dangers presented by the huge pond. She said, "Boy, they need to build a fence around the pond and put in some kind of an alarm system that lets them know when anyone is close. Maybe they can even have the boys wear sensors that will let them know when the boys are more than 50 feet from the house!" She was very sincere in her worry about the safety of my cherished grandsons.

I think my response shocked her, but it really gets at the core of Rule 1. I told her that they didn't need to build any fences or install any alarms: "Teach them to swim!" was my simple reply. The ultimate protection against water for children lies in teaching them to swim, not in keeping them away from water. Water is everywhere! You protect them by teaching them to swim.

The same is true for protecting kids from drugs. We'll never be able to remove drugs completely from their environment, so we must arm them with training on what to do when they are offered drugs. Just like protecting them from water, we must "teach them to swim," and teach them how to stay afloat in their world. Positive ideas give kids the ability to "swim" through the tough world they'll grow up in.

Chapter 6

Rule Two: Criticize the Performance, Not the Person

When I was growing up on our cattle ranch in the little town of Ellensburg, Washington, I was fortunate to be in the constant presence of Buck Minor, one of the most amazing men I have ever been privileged to know. Even today, Buck is one of my greatest heroes and role models. Buck has an amazingly intuitive way of teaching. This rule is a direct outgrowth of what I learned when I took a closer look at the effective teaching skills of this great American cowboy.

A Cowboy's Wisdom

I remember very clearly one experience I had with Buck when I was just seven. (I didn't understand the lesson of his wisdom until years later, when I looked back on the experience with a new perspective.) One day, as I walked through our barn with Buck, he put his arm around me and said, "Well, kid, it's about time for you to have a man's job here on the ranch. Most kids couldn't handle this kind of work until they were about 10, but you seem to be ready, so I'm going to give you a real job to do every day."

Buck Minor taught me to play the harmonica and a lot more. Who were your role models while growing up? Are you guiding your children to select their role models carefully? These people will have amazing power in guiding your children's decision-making.

I couldn't wait to get to work because of the way Buck presented this work opportunity. He didn't start off by talking about the job. He started off by talking about me and his confidence in my ability to do the job. He gave me a buildup first. Because he expressed his confidence in my ability to do the job, I began by focusing on success, too. He placed in my head an expectation of success and a delight in doing a good job.

Then Buck gave me the job: "You'll be in charge of cleaning out the two horse stalls over here." Wow! I couldn't wait to get started! This man had just told me that I was unique, and worthy of doing a man's work—I was going to get to shovel horse manure!

Think about this for a minute! A man had just given a seven-year-old child the job of shoveling horse poop out of the barn; and the kid couldn't wait to get started! Because of the way Buck had presented the job, the important thing to me wasn't that the job was shoveling horse poop, but that he had presented the job in a manner that caused me to *choose* to do it—happily.

Even though I wouldn't realize it until years later as I reflected back on it, Buck taught me a life lesson in that simple act: *People must be recognized as worthwhile in any request for action.* By recognizing me as a worthwhile person, he could ask me to do a distasteful job, and I'd feel great self-worth in doing it.

As I reflect back on that day, I realize that Buck taught me something else as he assigned me that ugly task. After giving me this job, this amazing man then *let me do it.* He didn't hang over my shoulder continually: He let me do it the way I saw fit. Then, after letting me do the job for a couple weeks, Buck offered a critique that produced more positive results.

One day he again put his arm over my shoulder and walked me to the horse stalls. "Kid," he said, "you have really been doing a great job cleaning out these stalls. You haven't missed a day. Most kids couldn't handle a job like this. Even kids much older than you would have taken a couple days off and needed some nagging, but you didn't." Privately, I knew I had missed a couple days, but because of Buck's praise and confidence in me, I knew I would never disappoint him again.

Now came the real lesson. He had shown me how to get a kid to do an unpleasant job by letting me feel worthwhile. Next, he wanted to get some improvement in my performance, and it was time for criticism. Buck shared a belief with my grandfather, who often said, "That criticism is best when it sounds like an explanation." So here's how he did it. After walking me through the barn with his arm over my shoulder and complimenting me for the fine work, he simply said, "Oh, by the way, most of the cowboys get the stuff in the corners, too," and he walked away.

Buck had just told me that I wasn't doing a very thorough job of shoveling horse poop, but I received the criticism as a piece of advice that I could choose to use to improve my standing as a man! He did not make the criticism the total focus of his comments. He complimented me on the work I had done, then made an offhand comment, and in so doing made it palatable to me.

Buck gave me a buildup first, then criticized my performance in a manner that allowed me not only to accept it but use it to do a better job in the future.

From Our Barn to Your House

How might you use this with your kids? Let's say you have a task in your home that you would like to have your child perform—perhaps mowing the lawn or taking out the garbage. First, do like Buck and give the task to your child with ample instruction. Explain how to do the job in behavioral terms that they clearly understand. Show the child how to start the mower, do the trimming, and operate the grass catcher. Have the kid pick up the garbage, carry it out to the outdoor garbage can, and put the garbage in it. While explaining the job, be sure to comment on how much you admire them for being able to handle this necessary job and how much you appreciate their cheerful attitude in accepting the job and helping around the home.

After they clearly understand the job, let them do it on their own a few times. Then, while complimenting them on the nice job they've done, offer any criticisms you may have—but only of the *performance*, not the *kid*. Something like, "By the way, I forgot to show you, but if you get the grass under the hedges, it'll make the job really look sharp," or "When you take the garbage out, it really makes the kitchen a nicer smelling and healthier place if you swish the can out with the hose before bringing it back in the house."

There are also applications of this rule that have a broader effect than just getting chores done! If you're trying to get your kids to be kind to each other, you might pick a quiet moment with your oldest child to point out three situations when she was kind or helpful to her little brother or sister. Compliment her and tell her how much you respected her and how it really showed how grownup she was becoming. You've just given her some positive thoughts or images of herself: times when she has risen to the level of your expectations about being nice to a younger sibling.

Your criticism will then come as a simple suggestion about future behavior, a way for her to keep earning the respect she's basking in right now. "You know, one of the best ways to make your little brother feel important is for you to play one of your games with him. He has an attention span of about three minutes, but if you just invite him to play with you, in three minutes you'll make a friend for life out of him. When you're through playing, be sure you say, 'Thanks, Sam. I really liked playing with you. Let's do it again tomorrow!'"

Think about this for a minute. It's easy to frown and say to your oldest daughter, "You never play with your brother!" This may be true, but in pointing it out, you more firmly plant "never play with your brother"—and reinforce the negative behavior! By getting out of that negative cycle, you put the focus on future behavior and turn criticism into positive suggestions that really improve performance!

As a teacher, I found many applications for this rule, but I had to be on guard to make sure I truly used it positively. In one freshman English class, I had an angry young man who really could not write. He could spell few words correctly and had almost no knowledge of proper sentence structure. My natural inclination was to parrot his teachers of the preceding nine years and just tell him he couldn't write. But once I identified this rule about criticizing the performance and not the person, I decided to be more purposeful in my approach.

One day the young man made an angry comment about a reading assignment in Shakespeare's *Romeo and Juliet*. His comment was actually thoughtful and insightful, so as he was on the way out of class, I called him up to my desk and said, "Wow, Todd, that was a very thoughtful comment you made. The students in my other classes could really benefit from your wise comment. It's a shame they won't be able to hear it."

"Why can't they?" he asked.

"Because they weren't in this class, and you have a hard time putting your ideas on paper. How would you like some help writing that idea down so I can share it with my other classes?"

The young man amazed me when he replied, "I would love some help writing it down. That's the first time any teacher has ever been interested in what I have to say!"

We began meeting in the morning before school to write and expand upon his idea, and these sessions soon blossomed into a long process of teaching him how to write coherently. Within two years, he had become a skilled writer and his paper was picked as one of the top five papers in the junior year writing assessment for the school district. He is now studying to be an English teacher!

It all started by imitating the teaching style of a cowboy named Buck Minor. Try it out and see if you can have similar success with your children. It might seem like a small, semantic difference between telling a kid he's messy and telling him he has the ability to be tidy, and you're surprised by the mess he just made, but it's a very important difference.

To this day my mom and I laugh about this very scenario. Ninety-nine percent of the advice my mother gave us kids was upbeat and positive, but one thing she said to me over and over while I was growing up is still sharp in my mind today. I can still see her standing in the doorway to my bedroom saying, "Messy, messy, messy. Oh, Mac, you are so messy!" And then, as if this weren't enough for me to get it, she'd say, "And you made such a mess in the barn today, too. It's no wonder you can't find your baseball mitt, because you leave it all over the place!"

I can remember repeating her comments over and over to myself. I repeated it to the point that by age four, I felt like shouting, "Mom, you don't need to say that anymore. I've got it! *I am messy!*"

We still have new reasons to laugh about it. A year ago I went to visit her and got in after she was in bed. The next morning I heard her rustling around in the kitchen, fixing coffee, so I got up and went out to read the paper and enjoy a little morning coffee and conversation with my beloved mother. She placed a cup of coffee in front of me and then, as she walked past the door to her guest room, she looked in and laughed, "Oohhh, I did such a good job! I see you're still doing just what I said when you were a kid. You've only been here for about six hours and your room is already messy!"

Now that we both have new parenting tools and rules to use, she and I both know that it would have been so much easier if she had just stopped and used a different approach. She told me I was messy hoping that I would see my mess and change. But I didn't. Instead, I listened to her and accepted her comment as fact. "I am messy."

If she had simply said, "Mac, it surprises me that a young man with your intelligence and organizational skills would let his room be just a big pile of stuff. I would think that a bright kid like you would organize your clothes just like they go on your body, with your T-shirts in the top drawer, your underwear in the next drawer, your pants in the next, and your socks in the bottom drawer. It also surprises me that you would organize your books in a pile, rather than having all of your horse books in one group, your mysteries in another, your adventure stories in another, and your scouting books in another. Or at least organize them by size from the biggest books on down to the smallest. Or it would seem that it might have occurred to you to group them by author in alphabetical order."

You see, in the time it took for her to scold me for being messy, she could have explained the course of action she *wanted* me to follow, while at the same time letting me know that she believed in my capabilities. Taking the time to *show me* her organizational ideas, with both of us rearranging clothing or restacking books, would have been the best combination of creating a new idea in my own head for my new "neater" behavior.

It's important for me to note here that I'm not sitting around blaming my mother for my shortcomings. Quite the contrary. It is amazing to me to look back at all the things my mother taught me how to do. She taught me to believe in myself and to take on big challenges. She taught me that it was okay for a man to cry, and that it was a strong man who could love his children openly. She taught me to feel empathy for people in tougher situations than mine. Above all, she taught me to love life and to soak in all that it had to offer. She taught me all of this and much more by painting positive pictures in my head of all the possibilities she could see for me. Because she only criticized my performance as she was painting this picture, I was able to accept her criticism as a way to improve myself. I wish every kid could have a mom just like mine.

In your family, think of instances where you can place a positive picture of excellent performance in your children's heads rather than simply criticizing what they've done wrong. Every mistake then becomes a teaching opportunity for you and an opportunity for improvement for them. Of course, some changes come more quickly than others, but then nobody said this was *easy!*

Chapter 7

Rule Three: Don't Assume They Learned It: *Repeat It!*

Almost everyone knows that repetition is fundamental to any learning experience. But when we begin teaching our children we seem to forget that fact! Rule 3 aims at correcting that oversight.

If we want our children to learn something, most of the time it will require some repetition of the concept! Repetition will be even more necessary if the idea we want them to master is a complex one. If you have a particular religious belief you wish to have your children adopt as the guiding force in their lives, you will need to repeat the concepts and teachings of that religion. Your children won't master your religious beliefs in a half an hour of Sunday School once a week. They need to hear you discussing those concepts almost daily at the dinner table. They need to hear you discussing those concepts as you watch TV together, and they darned sure need to see you *using* them on a daily basis as you make critical decisions in your life. Show them that those religious beliefs help you make critical decisions during tough times and happy times. Repetition, repetition, repetition! If you tell them that your religion is a source of joy, then they had better see you become happier as a result of prayer.

There are a couple things to remember as you repeat concepts for your children. First, it is necessary to guard against *repetition* becoming just *nagging*. Simply saying something over and over is not the same thing as *teaching*, and your kids hearing something over and over is not the same thing as *learning*. You have to tie all kinds of experiences, examples, and applications into the constant repetition of important ideas and concepts.

If you tell your children, "Honesty is the best policy," they need to see you practicing honesty in many situations and see it bringing about positive results for you, them, and others. They need to experience lots of opportunities to practice honesty in their own lives.

Dick and Maxine Matthews, Barbara's parents, taught our family to honor commitments. Here they are with Drew at his high school graduation, their ever-present smiles showing their pride and love. In the lives of our children, they showed up; they were involved. They showed all of us that love is a participatory sport. Are you showing up in your kids' lives? Do you smile and laugh with them daily?

When It's Time to Say It Differently

When using repetition, always remember the Rule of Three: "If you've said something three times and the person still isn't doing what you said, it's time to change the words!" We travel the country and we hear one statement more often than you would believe. With some variations, the statement goes, "If I've told Billy once, I've told him a thousand times!"

Now, there is a slow learner in every one of those situations, but it is *not* Billy! Doesn't it stand to reason that if you've said something to someone a thousand times and they're still not doing it, then those words simply aren't working? Might it be necessary, just maybe, to change the way you're presenting the idea?

When you have an important idea that you wish to have your children learn as a guiding principle in their lives, it must be repeated. If they don't seem to be learning or using the idea to make positive decisions, you may have to say it a different way. In fact, try a completely different manner of presentation. If you said it first, then it may be a good idea to write it, or you might try role-playing it to demonstrate the idea. You might even create an activity where the concept must be used in a real situation.

A couple years ago while I was teaching our Parenting with Dignity course in Yakima, Washington, I got to this point in my presentation, and I noticed a quiet gentleman who suddenly seemed to have an idea and began writing. I didn't ask him about it at the time, and it was almost six weeks later when he offered his first comment to the class, about changing the manner of repeating an important concept. He had always seemed more comfortable listening and learning quietly, but on this particular evening he seemed anxious to share something with us.

"A few weeks ago," he began, "I heard the rule on repetition and that it's important to change the way you're presenting something if you've said it more than three times, and a light seemed to go on in my head. I realized I had been repeating something over and over for my family, but because I was simply *saying* it, my repetition had just become nagging. I needed to find another way to teach the concept—it was time to say it with different words and a practical demonstration!

"I thought I was the only person in my family who understood the simple concept that electricity costs money! My gosh, I would come home and all the lights in the house would be on. I would come to the back door and it would be wide open with the thermostat turned up to 78 degrees! The TV would be on—with nobody watching it. The second TV would be on with the video game playing itself and nobody in the room. I would walk into the kitchen and there would be my wife with the oven on and all of the burners going. When I asked her what she was doing, her reply was, 'My feet were cold!' I would go through the house turning off the lights, and it would seem there was a ghost right behind me, turning them on again!

"I kept saying, 'Does anyone else in this family realize that electricity costs money?' It just seemed to fall on deaf ears. The kids would even say, 'Oh Dad, you're always saying that.'"

"I wasn't listening to them. And then, finally, I heard them. They weren't understanding what I was saying, so I decided to try saying it in a different manner.

"I first went to my bank and I opened a checking account in the name of my middle son, who's nine years old. When the checks were printed, I sat down with my son for a little talk. 'Son,' I began, 'these checks have your name on them. They work just like money. All you have to do is write the date here, the name of the person or business you're paying right here, the amount of money you're paying—in numbers—right here, and the amount of the money in words right here. Sign it at the bottom right here, and you can use this just like you would cash. You can buy burgers, video games, CDs, clothes, model airplanes—anything you want! And I want to show you another thing about your new checking account. See this part right here? This is called your register. It is where you can keep track of how much money you have and can spend. Right now it says $300. That's how much money I put into your account. Every month I will put $300 in your account, and that money will be yours to spend on anything you choose. Now, there is one thing that you will have to do every month—you will have to pay this.' And then I gave him the family electric bill!

"I was paying an average of around $240 every month. Now I was putting my son in charge of paying the electric bill, with some positive potential outcomes available to him. I told him, 'Son, remember, every dollar you don't spend on electricity, you can spend on anything you choose!'

"Man, I created a monster! That night I came home and sat down in my easy chair to read the newspaper and watch the news on TV. All of a sudden, my son came in and asked, 'Dad, what are you going to do: Read the paper or watch TV?'

"I responded, 'Well, I thought I would do both.'

"'You can't do both! Choose, which are you going to do?'

"'Well, I guess I'll read the paper.' Off went the TV, and every other light in the room but the little reading light he had put over my chair.

"Later that evening, I began to feel chilly. I went over to the thermostat and the thing was turned down to 62 degrees! I was just reaching to turn the heat up when I heard a voice shouting my own words at me: 'Hey, if you're cold, put on a sweater! Don't you have some slippers? And if you're still cold, move around, do a little exercise, it might do you some good as well as warming you up!'

"Then I went outside to get in the hot tub and it was cold! I came back in the house and shouted, 'Who turned the hot tub down?'

"'I did,' my son answered. 'You only use it once a week. Plan ahead and turn it up the morning of the day you want to sit in it. No point in heating the thing all week just to sit in it for 10 minutes one night!'

"Wow," the father went on, "My son did, in one month, what I had not been able to do in 14 years of marriage! He had gotten our electric bill under $100! He now had $200 of spending money to use as he pleased.'

"I had simply said the same thing I'd been saying to him, but I said it in a different way! Look at the graphic result. (My only mistake was in giving him a $300 deposit in the first place!) I had said 'electricity costs money' in a way that he could finally hear it and apply it to his life! He could spend the money he saved on things that he wanted. He now knew that the real meaning of 'electricity costs money.' It cost him *his* money!"

Then this remarkable young father went on with a few more astute observations. "Not only did I get my son to understand that electricity is not free, I taught him some other important lessons that I also hadn't been teaching very effectively. I taught him that a family is a place where everyone participates! He suddenly became a real and active participant in our family in a very tangible way. Also, I had taught him that he was an amazingly capable young man. He could even do some things his dad couldn't do! And most important, I had taught my son that he was a valued person in the eyes of his father. He could not deny it. My actions said it in a way that he could not deny!"

In your family, are there lessons you're trying to teach your children, but you're simply not repeating the important ideas often enough? Are you repeating things but not doing it effectively? Are you letting your repetition become just background noise or even nagging? Can you think of ways that you might be able to say the same thing but in a different way, or demonstrate them to give them strong meaning for your children? Look for those teachable moments, and opportunities to say something graphically, in a different way.

One year while I was teaching a history class about the Holocaust, my students didn't seem to be getting it. Most seemed bored and uninterested. I realized that I needed to find another way for them to understand the significance of this dark period in human history.

After much thought, here is how I repeated the concepts in a different manner. I gave a surprise exam on the previous day's lesson. Then during the test, in preplanned five-minute intervals, I accused students of cheating and kicked them out of class, declaring that they would receive zeroes on the test and probably be suspended from school without credit for three days. (I had a counselor in the hall waiting to catch these kids, and it was a good thing I did, too, because a couple were so angry that they were actually crying because of the injustice of being wrongfully accused of cheating.)

I had chosen the kids I would accuse the night before. I began with a couple kids everyone might expect to be cheating, but then I picked a couple of good students with reputations for honesty.

The first couple kids left the room with little question or argument. When I got to one of the students who would never cheat, she challenged me, but I simply yelled at her to leave the room. The next student I accused was appalled that I would actually suspect him, but he left the room quietly. Finally, I chose a young lady who was the best student in class and had straight A's through her entire three years of high school. She began to cry when I tore up her test. It was all I could do to keep up with my act.

Then I asked the rest of the class to put down their pens and pencils and stop working on their tests. I went out into the hall and asked all the students accused of cheating to return to the room. When all the kids were back, I asked the class a couple questions. "How many of you stood up to defend your classmates?" None raised their hands.

Then I asked, "For those of you who were not kicked out, what did you do when you saw your friends being kicked out?"

Most of them replied that they just tried to get closer to their desks and be sure they did nothing to get kicked out.

Next, I asked the students who had been wrongfully accused, "What did you think as you were being sent out of the class for something you did not do?"

"I just planned to talk to the principal and have him fix it," replied the straight-A student who had left the room crying. One of the boys said that he was thinking he would get his dad to bring a lawyer to school to plead his case.

"And what would you have done if all those people were corrupt or at least backed the teacher who was abusing his power?"

Then I began to make some comparisons between their actions and what happened during the Holocaust. "Yesterday, you all said it was really stupid that the German people let the Nazi Party take over their country and start hauling the Jews off to concentration camps. You all said that you would have stood up for the people being innocently hauled away in the middle of the night. But today when you saw your friends being wrongfully accused, not one of you spoke up. Do you understand a little bit more about what it's really like when power is abused? It can even happen to you. Now I would like each of you to stop and think a little bit, then try to put your ideas on paper for tomorrow."

Boy, did I receive some thoughtfully written papers the next day. I had found another way to explain how the Holocaust had happened. I had not just repeated the same thing in the same way. Can you think of some new and different ways you can communicate some of the ideas you have been attempting to teach your children?

We have always tried to find unique ways to repeat ideas to our kids. From the time our kids were just beginning to talk, before they could really understand the words, I have continually stressed to them the importance of honesty. I tried to describe it in terms that they could understand. "Say what you mean, mean what you say, and then do what you say you're going to do!" I said it so many times I sounded like a broken record even to myself, but there were still times when I tried to find other ways to teach honesty to them, ways where actions spoke louder than words.

For example, one day I was at the grocery store with one of our sons and I paid for a few groceries with two $10 bills. The cashier gave me my $12 worth of groceries—and then she gave me $18 and some change. As we were going out to the car I got to adding up what had just happened. The lady had made just about exactly a $10 mistake. Realizing what had happened I said to my son, "Look at this, that lady must have given me back one of my $10s by mistake. We have to go back in and give it back to her!"

Our son's reaction was quick and natural, especially in light of how honesty is portrayed in so many places in the world today. He said, "No way, Dad! She made the mistake. You've got the money, and if you don't want to keep it, I will."

"No, son, remember what I have always told you: Honesty is always the best policy!" So we went back in to the cashier, showing her my change, my receipt, and my groceries.

"Oh my gosh," she said, "I made a mistake! I accidentally gave you back one of your $10s! Thank you, thank you, thank you! If you hadn't come back, I would have had to make up the shortage in my cash drawer out of my own pocket. I had to make up a $20 mistake just yesterday, and I can't afford another $10 mistake today. I don't know how to thank you."

We walked out and I just said, "Son, you wait, the honesty of today will come back to benefit us some day."

I forgot all about it, and I'm sure our son did, too. Then, about three weeks later, we were in a hurry to catch a plane and I realized I had forgotten to go to the bank and get some cash for the trip. The bank was closed and I didn't have a card for the cash machine, so on the way to the airport I ran into the grocery store. My son was with me when I got to the cash register and I said to the checker, "I know it's your store policy to only cash a check for $20 over the amount of purchase, but I was wondering if you could waive that policy tonight, because—"

The lady interrupted me and said, "Write your check for whatever amount you want, Mr. Bledsoe—I'll vouch for you with my boss if there's any problem!" It was the same lady to whom I had returned the $10!

I wrote a check for $300 and went out to the car with our son. "Did you see that, son? My face just cashed a check. I didn't even have to show my ID. All she had to do was see my face and she was willing to bend the rules to help me out. Honesty *is* the best policy. I was honest with her a few weeks ago, and it just came back to me tonight. If you conduct yourself with honesty, it will almost always come back to you in a much bigger way."

There is another thing that I have tried to teach to our sons via repetition. Since before they could understand the words I have been telling them, "It is Bledsoes against the world." I would whisper it in their ears when I would tuck them into their cribs when they were babies. As they grew up I kept on saying the same words: "It is Bledsoes against the world." Many times I didn't think they understood what I was saying. I tried to show them by my actions that, no matter what, I was on their side in life, but I still wasn't sure they understood me. Finally, about four years ago, I had belt buckles made for each of them, with those words inscribed on them. Barbara thought it was a good idea, so she had one made for me. That same year I had one made for Barbara and gave it to her on our anniversary. This year for Christmas, we had one made for Drew's wife, Maura. This year we intend to have buckles made for our grandkids.

However, it is interesting how something like that can become one of the ideas that rule our world. I experienced one of my biggest tragedies a year ago in February, when my best friend, John Matau, finally lost a five-year battle with intestinal cancer. He had been my best friend almost from the day we met some 32 years ago. It was a terrible loss to the world when John died, because he was the best and most amazing schoolteacher I have ever met. He might have been the best who ever lived. His death came right on the heels of the death of Barbara's father, who had died a month earlier. Only three months prior to that, another of my best friends, Bobby Dunnington, had been killed suddenly, right in the prime of life, in a terrible motorcycle accident. I was devastated by all of this tragedy. In retrospect, I know I have lived a gifted existence to have avoided tragedy for most of my life, but I was devastated by these sudden deaths so close to my heart.

In a few short months, the people whom I most often sought out for laughter were gone. Bobby laughed more than any other human being I had ever known. He attacked life with such a love of living that he inspired me to always do new things and find new ways to have fun.

John was the funniest person I had ever known. We had a friendship forged in laughter and built on a common and fiercely held philosophy of teaching young people out of love, respect, and the dignity of always holding them to high standards of performance.

Barbara's father, Dick Matthews, was perhaps my biggest hero, for the unswerving manner in which he honored commitments. His death had further emptied my life, and I felt sort of rudderless during these months of personal loss. Time has allowed me to put these events in perspective, but at the time I was emotionally depleted like I have never been before or since.

I had been asked to give the eulogy at the huge memorial service for my buddy John, a man so universally loved by so many families that his memorial service had to be held in the Walla Walla High School Gymnasium. He had touched so many lives with his amazing and loving existence. I was so shaken by the past few months that I wasn't sure I could give my planned talk. I had worked it out with the minister conducting the service that if I was feeling too unsteady I would just give him a sign, and he would simply read in my place a written statement I had given him. I didn't want to embarrass everyone at the service by completely falling to pieces trying to deliver the eulogy.

I had never felt so unsure of myself, and I was just about to give him the sign. It was nearing my point to speak during the service when I felt two big strong hands grab each of my arms. At my greatest moment of weakness, my two sons were each grabbing one of my arms. Drew leaned over while holding my arm and whispered into my ear, "Come on, Dad, nobody can tell them about your amazing buddy John like you can!"

Then Adam, squeezing my other arm, whispered in my other ear, "Come on, Dad, just like you always said, 'It is Bledsoes against the world!' We're going up there with you, and we'll do this together!"

And then those two big young men—our sons—almost physically picked me up and carried me to the podium. As we were walking up to the podium, they said, "We're here to support you, but we know you can do this for your buddy!"

In my moment of greatest need, I finally came to know the true meaning of the words I had been saying to my kids for years. I, too, finally came to know what it means when we say to each other, "It is Bledsoes against the world."

Take it from me, whatever you give to a child will come back to you 10 times over. If you do a good job in teaching a worthwhile concept to your children, they will probably come back and teach it to you with new meaning. Repeating worthwhile ideas is worth it! Decide on the most meaningful ideas that you would have rule the world of your children, then repeat them to your kids in as many ways as you can. The more that you repeat the key ideas, the greater the chance those same ideas will become the ideas that rule their worlds!

Chapter 8

Rule Four: What They Say to Themselves Is What Counts

When I started teaching, I was fresh out of the Army, and let me say that the two years I spent in that organization were not the most positive times in my life. I saw enough negative and punitive tactics in the Army to last me three lifetimes, so I began my teaching career determined never to resort to negative reinforcement. If I didn't believe in negative reinforcement, then I must be in favor of positive reinforcement! I believed I was going to change the world with "attaboys" and "waytagos."

I actually thought I was going to teach by slapping everyone on the back and change behavior by congratulating everyone on their good work. Man, was I in for a surprise! Positive reinforcement didn't seem to be much more effective in changing behavior than negative reinforcement. It did seem to me that concepts and procedures kids learned when I used positive reinforcement remained with them longer, but that was just a feeling; I really couldn't quantify it. Granted, I felt better for not being negative, and I think my students also felt much more at ease in my class, since they didn't have to listen to a bunch of scolding and negative rhetoric—but they didn't seem to be learning much more or performing much better.

What You Say vs. What They Hear

Then I learned a valuable lesson that has stuck with me. I had been under the impression that what I said was exactly what kids heard and stored in their script about themselves. I learned that I was operating under a real fallacy!

More often than not, I would say something like, "Nice job on the paper you turned in today; you really did a wonderful job of writing!" assuming the student heard exactly what I said. But gradually I began to realize I was mistaken. Often, what they would say to themselves was far different, more like, "No, it wasn't a good job! I copied the whole thing from the encyclopedia; you just didn't catch me!" What I had intended to be a positive statement on the student's performance had been stored in their mind as a negative! I said, "Nice job!" What the student stored—whether he felt good or bad about it—was, "I'm a cheat!"

The two statements could not be more different and—more important—the two statements have opposite effects upon future performance.

I had discovered an important truth about shaping my students' behavior and performance, but I didn't have a clue how to use it. So I began to try different ways of *using* my newfound knowledge. First, I tried to structure situations to get students to repeat positive statements out loud. For example, I was teaching a remedial math class and began every class by having the students read out loud a slogan I had on a poster at the front of the room: "There is no mystery in math. Math is a set of simple and logical rules, and I know how to apply them." Then every time a student would express confusion or frustration, I would have him read the statement out loud again before I would give him an answer or give him help. It worked for some kids, but many seemed to interpret it as an embarrassing, annoying repetition or nagging.

Finally, I realized that it was foolish to treat all kids in the same way. What an important concept: All kids are not the same! The techniques that worked for some kids didn't work for others, and I had to find ways to get *every* student thinking positive things about himself and his unique abilities. I discovered that for some kids it simply took longer, and for others I had to search more diligently for the right tactics.

I had discovered that positive statements really were more effective in shaping kids' behavior, but only if the kids heard and repeated to themselves those positive statements.

Tricked into Excellence

My buddy John Matau, whom I have already mentioned in this book, was a master at tricking kids into self-discovering positive ideas about themselves. Here is one example of his amazing skill as a teacher that you may be able to imitate as you work with your own kids.

Almost every year, John would have what he called his "Cheater's Test" in his U.S. history classes. He would announce to his classes that, on the upcoming chapter test, he was going to challenge everyone to figure out a way to cheat and not get caught.

He laid out the rules very carefully. "You can cheat on this test, and if you get away with it, you get the score you get. However, if you get caught, it will be no different from other tests: You will receive a zero. *But*, unlike other tests, if you get caught cheating, you will be able to take the test again the next day. You'll have to live with whatever score you get on the second test! I will not call you a cheater, and you will not go to the office or receive any negative consequences for cheating other than having to take the test a second time.

"You will have exactly 55 minutes to complete the test. During the test, I will leave the room one time. I will be gone for exactly 30 seconds. The rest of the time, I will sit at my desk and read a book, except for three times when I will get up and walk around the room. Get creative! On the 'Cheater's Test,' if you don't get caught, you get to keep your score!"

My buddy John Matau taught me to dream of a better world for kids, that laughter was a powerful teaching tool, and that every kid had good in them and it was our job to find it. Who are those amazing teachers in your life? In your children's?

On test day, it was amazing to watch the creativity of the kids. Excitement would be at a fever pitch throughout the school as the kids tried to match wits with John and outdo each other with their schemes. What was interesting was that the kids who hooked in on this opportunity the most were usually kids who were failing or close to it! Some would have friends in the gym reading the answers on a walkie-talkie, with three students sitting in class listening on earphones hidden behind long hair. Others would have the answers written on the bottom of their shoes. Others would have elaborate mechanisms that would retract the cheat sheet into their sleeve when they straightened their arm. Groups would get together and hide answers around the room on the backs of lights and on bulletin boards. Some would put the answers on the front of John's desk. Their creative minds were hard at work!

The day after the "Cheater's Test," John would give the test again, as planned, for any kids who had been caught cheating. He also asked everyone else to take the test, saying he just wanted to see what happened. He told them that if they scored higher today, they could keep the higher score. The scores would almost universally average in the 80s and 90s! Even kids who had never passed a test in their lives would get 94s and 88s.

The self-discovery would begin when John would point out something to his classes. "Kids, you learned something today. Many of you scored higher than you've ever scored on a test in your life, and *today* you did it without cheating. Do you know how you did that? Well, for yesterday's test, you had to make up your elaborate cheat sheets. In order to do that, you had to actually look up the answers to what you thought would be on the test and write them down! Many of you even wrote the answers two or three times as you perfected your cheating schemes.

"Now look at what you did today! You scored very highly on today's test with nothing but what you stored in your head by looking up the answers and writing them down. What you did while preparing to cheat is what many people call *studying!* You did what many students who get good grades do before a test. It wasn't very hard was it? It also didn't take much time, either, did it?

"Now recall what it felt like to take this test today and score highly. Pretty cool, huh? Why don't you do that all the time, since you just demonstrated to yourself that you can do it?"

John had just tricked many kids into saying some pretty positive things to themselves about their performance capabilities. The key is that he got them to say it for themselves after giving them a graphic experience with their own performance.

Teaching with Dignity

John Matau was a champion of the "wayward" kids in every school where he taught. He worked to give every kid a chance to be the best he could possibly be. He was also a dreamer. He had the audacity to dream of a school built to actually meet the needs of kids rather than the needs and convenience of adults. John Matau also had the audacity to act upon his dreams. About six years before his untimely death, he had the guts to build just such a school—and you know what? He succeeded!

The school was called the Opportunity Program, and it was located in the little rural town of Walla Walla, Washington. He built it in space he rented in the basement of an old church, using no special funds or grants, just state funding for public schools. His school started at 6 in the morning and closed at 11 at night. The goal was to have a school that would meet the needs of kids who had to have jobs in order to live.

The school district gave John the privilege of attempting to start the school, and that was amazing enough. But few people in the district held much hope of John's actually succeeding. He was told that he could not recruit students from the regular high school or from the alternative high school. He had to find his students in the "dropout" population of high school age kids on the streets of Walla Walla.

Now, Walla Walla is a town of about 30,000 people, but almost immediately the enrollment at the Opportunity Program grew to between 195 and 205 full-time students! Many were amazed that John was able to find that many kids on the streets of that little town, and even more amazed that he was able to entice them to register, attend classes, and earn credits at his Opportunity Program. Soon the enrollment demanded that the school move into larger facilities, so they moved into part of an old grocery store, which John and his amazing staff remodeled into a nice school.

It was pretty easy to see how John built such a successful school and attracted so many kids who had left the traditional system. All you had to do was visit the school. He structured an environment that recognized the dignity and worth of every student. When new students would drop in to investigate this school they had heard other kids talk about or that John had described in his visits to their hangouts, he would meet them at the door and escort them into his office as if they were some business executive. He would get out his calendar and schedule a meeting with them sometime in the next week. He would write the date and time on an appointment card with his phone number on it, telling the new prospect that if the time became difficult for them to just give him a call and they would reschedule it for a more convenient time. Then he would instruct the student to come to the appointment and to bring her "best self"! "When you come, dress in the way that you feel most comfortable and that you think shows the world the best you that is possible. That doesn't mean that you have to dress like me."

When the prospective student would come for the appointment, John would take her around and introduce her to the entire staff as if he were entertaining the governor of the State of Washington! He didn't tell the student about the teachers—he told the teachers about the student. This was a subtle difference, but most students at the Opportunity Program would later share that this was the first time that any of them had ever been treated as a valued person in a school setting!

Then John would take the candidate into his office, where he would conduct a lengthy interview that resembled a recruiting session of a large business or law firm. He would talk with the student about her personal goals, educational goals, and career goals, and he would write these goals down on a form. Then he would present the student with a contract to sign, simply confirming her intent to enroll at the Opportunity Program and put forth her best effort in attempting to reach her goals. As soon as the interview was completed, he would have one of his staff take the student's picture with a digital camera.

Immediately, before the student was allowed to leave, a poster of the photo was created to go on a wall of the school called the "Wall of Fame." The photo was put up right there with the pictures of every other student in the school. Under the picture was the student's name, one of her personal goals, one of her educational goals, and one of her career goals. He was careful to have the student's permission to use each of these goals, so as not to violate her privacy.

As the student was getting ready to leave, everyone on the staff would come out and shake her hand, welcoming her to the Opportunity Program and congratulating her for taking this positive step toward a productive, fulfilling future.

Students were enrolled in one class at a time. They would work at their own speed until the class requirements were met, then they would enroll in a new class. Credits were earned one at a time, one course at a time. At the end of every day, the staff was required to say the name of each student in the school by looking only at pictures of them. The staff was required to share positive statements about their students with other staff members at weekly meetings, so they could all congratulate the kids by name every time they saw them.

What John Matau and his staff were doing was really pretty simple. They were getting kids to value themselves by treating them like they were valued rather than waiting for the kids to "earn" respect. They were getting kids to say it for themselves because of the way they were treated. He was operating on the premise that kids must say positive things about themselves to themselves, and that the best way to get them to do that was to treat them as valued people!

The cornerstone of the Opportunity Program's curriculum was that the school and its staff would uphold the highest possible standards. John went to the traditional high school and adopted their curriculum and evaluation standards for his amazing school. The Opportunity Program did not lower its standards for anyone. If the student earned her diploma and graduated, she had risen to the highest possible standard of performance.

Some people in the district were skeptical at first. Many doubted that what John was attempting was possible. Few believed that a school could demand high standards of students who had formerly failed at school and had dropped out. Understandably, some teachers from the traditional high school came to challenge the Opportunity Program. Many of these doubters who came to the school saw pictures of kids that they'd had in class in the past and became even more skeptical. It was fun to watch John greet them cheerfully at the door and invite them in for a tour. He would introduce his students to these visiting teachers, but it was the students who were introduced like dignitaries not the teachers. Invariably, John would invite them to come over any time to grade papers and help his staff evaluate the work of his students in order to uphold the high standards of the Walla Walla School System! He would cheerfully say, "Hey, we work on the portfolio method of record keeping, so any time anyone wants to see the progress of any of our students, we will gladly pull the student's portfolio. You can go through the student's work and see every assignment, paper, test, or project. This is how we hold our students to our extremely high standards!"

I think you can see how you might do a similar thing with your own kids. Explain to your children that your family holds them to extremely high standards of performance, manners, and personal grooming because they are exceptionally capable kids!

How would you conduct business with highly capable people? You would give them jobs of responsibility and importance. Do the same with your kids in your home. Give them a fixed amount of money and then have them do the grocery shopping for the month. Have them plan trips when the family travels. Let them set departure times and arrival times. Give them the map and have them select the best routes. Put them in charge of important tasks in the home and then let them figure out the best way to do the job.

The goal is for your kids to discover that they are valued and respected people because they are treated as such, and to say it for themselves. Be ready to offer feedback on their performance that will allow them to see how well they are doing, and how they could do even better. Kids learn much more from our back side than they do from our front side! They learn far more from how we treat them than from what we say, especially if we are given to exaggeration in our praise. Don't just tell them—*show them!*

Getting Positives into Their Heads

So now you're asking, "How can we use this rule in raising our children?" It can be an extremely powerful tool as children grow up, but it does require careful observation. It can be difficult to know what kids are saying to themselves, but, if we listen and watch carefully, with all of our parental perception, kids communicate what they're saying to themselves in some very tangible ways.

Listen carefully. When we say something to them that we consider to be encouragement, like, "I know that you can dress yourself," we must listen to what they say in response. Often their response will be something like, "No, I can't." We must listen to that comment! It does little good to ignore the statement and answer with something like, "Oh, yes you can." Remember, every time you tell them they can and they say they can't, they have just gotten another negative statement stored away in their script about their abilities and capability.

When a child says he can't do something, you have to create a situation or experience that gets him to learn and say something more positive. Get him to make positive statements about small parts of the activity. Sit down with the child and have him put on a pair of socks. Here is the critical step: Ask him to tell you what he just did. It might sound like this:

"Wow, what did you just do?"

"I put my socks on."

"Wow, that was well done. Can you tell your brother (or mom, dad, sister, brother, grandma, etc.) what you just did?"

"Daddy, I just put my socks on all by myself."

Look closely at what just happened. The child actually said, "I can put on my socks by myself," three times. First, when he put on his socks, second when he told you what he did, and third when he told someone else. The key to making this rule work lies in careful watching and listening, then seizing the opportunity to orchestrate a positive statement from the child about his or her own performance.

Never Stop Trying!

Our experience has been that at this point many parents say, "What do I do if my child doesn't say something positive when I set up the opportunity? We tried that and all she said was 'I can't do that!'"

My answer is always the same: Try again! Try it in another situation with another prompt. Keep up with the technique and *don't give up*. If you are just beginning to create these statements in your child and he or she is older, you may have years of negative statements to overcome. Sometimes it may take a long time to finally elicit a positive statement from a child—but once he starts, his confidence and positive attitude will keep him coming!

Let me share with you an experience that I had in teaching where a child overcame more negative statements than most kids ever have to deal with—and he did it with great success. He was one of my professors, and he taught me that the only time you fail with a child is the last time that you try!

I'll call this boy Bobby. He has given me permission to tell his story as long as I don't divulge his name or where he's from. When you hear the circumstances of his life, I think you'll see why he might be a bit hesitant to be identified with his history.

I met Bobby when he walked into my ninth-grade classroom on the first day of school. I immediately identified him as a boy who was going to be difficult to handle. He was hesitant to sit down at a desk, and during the first hour he continually got up and wandered around my classroom. He seemed unable to sit for more than a couple minutes, and parroted requests to sit down but didn't change his behavior. It would have been manageable to have him wandering around the classroom, but he seemed obsessed with starting arguments and instigating fights with other students.

This disruptive behavior went on for about a week until I was at my wits end. I had exhausted every technique I could think of, and I had repeated each one three or four times. Finally, sometime during the second week, I violated one of my standard procedures.

You see, I always told my students that they entered my classroom with a clean slate: I would judge them by what they did in my classroom, period. I would never go to counselors or other teachers and bias myself by learning their past. They would be judged and evaluated simply on the quality of their work and performance in my presence. This is how I would like to be treated. I would hate to have to make amends for every mistake I ever made before anyone gave me credit for my current work! So I tried to afford my students the same courtesy. It's important to note that many kids took this opportunity to rise way above past performance and even well above what past test scores would have predicted for their capabilities.

After I decided that this boy might have problems that I wasn't equipped to handle, I sought help from one of the school's most caring and trusted guidance counselors. After I briefly explained my dilemma, she took me into her office and closed the door. Then she went to her file cabinet and pulled out a file about as thick as a Tolstoy novel and set it on the desk. It was the file that had accompanied Bobby through his storied past in the school system.

For the next two hours, she laid out the problems and difficulties that this boy had been through. The file contained newspaper clippings that had been placed there by past counselors and from the Juvenile Detention Center. By his freshman year in high school, this young man had survived more than most adults would have been able to cope with. I know I would have given up after only half the hardships he had endured! I will cite only some of the "highlights" of his existence to that date.

At age nine, he witnessed his mother killing his three-year-old brother. His mother adamantly maintained that the little brother had been injured in a fall from a second-story stairway. She was charged with murder, but before the case went to trial the charges were dropped. The only evidence they had was Bobby's testimony, and her court-appointed attorney had informed both Bobby and his mother that his testimony was not admissible because he had testified before she had given permission, and he could not be forced to testify further against his mother. She was set free due to lack of evidence.

Bobby's mother was an alcoholic, and she had an alcoholic boy-friend who had lived in the home off and on for about four years. His idea of recreation was to go out and get drunk, then come home and beat on Bobby and his little brother and sister. Court investigations showed that there had been 11 or 12 such beatings, and on the final one Bobby had had enough. He came to the aid of his little sister and grabbed the man, beginning a fight that eventually moved into the front yard. The neighbors called 911, and when the police arrived Bobby was winning the fight. He was on top of the man, beating him with his fists, screaming, "I'll kill you! I'll kill you! I'll kill you!"

As a matter of fact, when Bobby calmed down at the police station, he refused his right to be silent and told them, "Yeah, I tried to kill him. Bring him in here right now and I'll try again!"

The live-in boyfriend swore out charges against Bobby for third-degree assault (which is defined as attempted murder), and Bobby stood trial. A number of the neighbors testified that Bobby seemed to be an extremely unruly child. They really felt that he was trying to kill that man that night, and they feared that he might be capable of it. Bobby was convicted and assigned to juvenile detention for a year. Upon his release, he was assigned to a foster home and had a restraining order placed on him that forbade him from being within a mile of his mother's house.

Bobby was currently living in his fifth foster home for that year. He had been removed from three of them because of his unruly behavior, instigating fights with the other children. He had been removed from the fourth not because he had done anything, but because the health department had closed it for poor "food sanitation conditions"!

The counselor told me that Bobby had all of his worldly possessions under his bed in a cardboard box. He refused to even put his stuff in dressers or closets because he wanted to be ready for the next move. Now I don't know about you, but I'm a fairly secure, self-confident person, and I'm not sure I could survive being moved to five different temporary homes in a year and having all of my "stuff" in a cardboard box! You may say that you might have learned the consequences of your own actions, but I doubt that I would have learned anything but bitterness and anger. Yet here was this boy attending my class every day.

My view of this young man changed rather markedly with this new information. All of a sudden I had a newfound respect for him! I was pretty amazed that he was able to function at even this level, given his background. As I said, I'm not sure I could have taken what he had and still been functioning at all. I made a personal commitment to be an advocate for this young man. I decided that I was going to be on his side. I went back to class determined to find some way to reach Bobby and teach him how to behave appropriately in a classroom.

A couple days went by and I hadn't yet made any progress, when a terrible thing happened. As nearly as I could reconstruct the sequence of events by talking with Bobby's classmates, things hadn't gone well for Bobby that tragic day. He had seemed unusually agitated in my class first period. When he arrived in his second period class, he had been even more unruly, and his second period teacher, in front of the whole class, had told him, "You know, Bobby, I have 154 kids in this classroom every day, and you are the only one that I am not glad to see!"

Like I said, I'm a pretty secure person, but I don't think I would have taken that insult. Bobby did.

(I want to say that I do understand how a teacher or parent can become frustrated enough to make a hurtful statement like that. It doesn't make it right, but sometimes statements that we don't mean can slip out. In working with kids, we must always keep in mind the destructive effect that a wayward angry comment made out of frustration can have on a child!)

Bobby went on to third period, where the teacher repeatedly scolded him for his unruly behavior. Then, in his fourth-period biology class, things hit the boiling point. His teacher apparently said something like, "Bobby, you worthless punk, you do nothing that I ask, get out of my room!"

Not to be outdone, Bobby shouted back, "You can't kick me out of your class because I quit!" and walked out the door with his middle finger raised. The teacher followed him into the hall, grabbed him by the back of the neck, and physically dragged him to the office. He told the principal, "This boy is to be removed from my class and he is not to be assigned to any other class. He is to be kept in the office this period and given a failing grade!"

That put the young man in a whole new type of trouble. One of the conditions of his parole from juvenile detention was that he had to maintain passing grades in five of his six classes. His math grade was already in jeopardy, so with a failing grade in biology, he was in violation of his probation.

He sat out the period in the office and went to fifth period, where halfway through the hour, a detention officer came into the room to get Bobby. Bobby immediately recognized the man and jumped up yelling, "You'll never take me!" A chase ensued, but after a minute the detention officer had the young man cornered. He tackled Bobby and pinned him to the floor, then with his knee on the back of Bobby's neck, the officer pulled his hands behind his back and handcuffed him, all in full view of his classmates. Then the officer yanked Bobby to his feet and virtually carried him kicking, screaming, and fighting from the classroom.

My first course of action after hearing these details from a student after school was to simply show up in person. I went down to the juvenile detention facility. It wasn't visiting hours, but I had been doing a lot of volunteer work with other kids in the facility, so I was allowed to get in to see Bobby. A guard escorted me to a part of the facility I had never been in. Bobby was being held in solitary confinement, in a cell reserved for inmates who are suicidal. Apparently, in the office after his arrest he made some self-destructive statements, and all suicide-prevention training says never to ignore suicidal comments. The facility was protecting Bobby by putting him in a padded cell and giving him a pair of orange prison pants with no drawstring and a pair of flip-flops. When I got to his cell he meekly walked out holding his pants up with one hand. When I saw him, all I could say was, "Hey, kid, you look like you could use a hug!" He ran to me and I pulled him to me. Man, he gripped me tight and wouldn't let go.

The guard said we couldn't just stand there in the hall, so he escorted us down to the visitor's room. It was a real friendly place with all of the furniture bolted to the floor, and we sat down at a table. Bobby grabbed my hand and wouldn't let go. I could empathize with that. If I were in his shoes, I think I would have needed some personal contact from someone, too.

As we were sitting there holding hands, I tried to communicate some important information to him. "Bobby," I said, "I want you to know that I am on your side. I have come here because I really care about you and I want to help you get through this. You can count on one thing from here on out, no matter what happens to you, and that is that I love you. I will show up and help you any time you need me to. When the sun comes up tomorrow, I am going to be on your side!"

We sat and talked for a while, then the guard came in and said I would have to leave because it was time for dinner. That tough little guy and I shared another long hug and he was escorted off to the chow hall. I watched through the wire-mesh glass as he went in to eat. He had a cardboard plate full of some unrecognizable food, a paper cup, and a "spork." I watched as he was seated, away from all of the other kids because he was a suicide risk, and again thought about how I would be doing if I were in his shoes. I don't know if I would have been able to hold up, but there, sitting all by himself, he looked up at me and smiled and waved. What a strong person! I became convinced that I had to do something concrete to help this boy.

As I was leaving the facility, the guard asked me to put my name on Bobby's visitor list so that I would not have to sign in every time I came. He took out a folder with Bobby's name on it and opened it. In the space marked "Visitors," Bobby had written the name of the only person he could think of who might come to visit him. In the space where he could write the names of as many as 20 visitors, he had written just one: mine! God save me if I hadn't shown up that day!

You know, it's an awesome thing we do when we take on a title like Mom, Dad, Teacher, Coach, or any other that kids bestow upon us. We have to be careful how we handle ourselves in these roles, because they carry with them an awesome investment of trust from those kids. Often we can desert kids right at the time when they need us most. When a kid upsets us with some silly, rebellious, or otherwise disappointing behavior, we must remember that we have the obligation to maintain the dignity in the situation. We have to show them another way, a positive way—not just dream up some consequence or punishment and then desert them. Most of the time, what they need is someone on their side to help them improve, not someone to punish them for what they did wrong!

I went home and tried to come up with a plan. The next day I visited Bobby first thing in the morning. I wanted him to know by my actions that I meant what I had said. Then, when I arrived at school, I began to take steps to get him back to school. I went to the biology teacher and got him to agree to let Bobby into another biology class with the passing grade he had before being kicked out. Once I had his permission, I found another teacher who would take Bobby into his class. Once he was reenrolled, it took almost three weeks to get him released because he was being subjected to lots of tests to evaluate his suicidal risk.

In the meantime, I decided to try to structure an environment of success for him at the school. I invited all of his teachers to join me for lunch to discuss a plan for him. I proposed to them that we could concoct a menu of consequences for Bobby's negative behavior, but we couldn't possibly duplicate the nasty consequences that had already been used to try to change him—all of which had failed!

His life to date was a monument to the fact that negative consequences didn't do anything to change negative behavior! So I proposed that we try a new approach. I suggested that we create a mental picture in our heads: Bobby is given a microchip recorder. It is attached to his shoulder and records every comment anyone makes about him. I asked them to imagine that, every night, Bobby plays back whatever is on the recorder. My proposal was that in the last five years of his life, I doubted that Bobby had more than a couple positive comments on his recorder. We needed to change that!

"Let's form a team to see if we can get some positive statements about Bobby on his recorder for him to replay! Here is what I suggest," I went on, just stabbing in the dark, really. "I've gotten each of us a whole bunch of Post-It notepads. Let's place them all around our rooms, and then let's try to catch Bobby doing something right! Every time you catch him sitting down, grab a notepad and write, 'Bobby, thanks for sitting down.' When you catch him with a pencil in his hand, write a note: 'Thanks for bringing a pencil to class.' When he speaks in a normal tone of voice, write, 'Thanks for speaking quietly!' I know we can do it because I've done it before, and it doesn't interrupt class."

When Bobby came back to school, we went to work, and slowly but surely, we began to notice more and more positive behavior to make comment upon. Our notes began to say things like "Thanks for turning in that assignment," or "Thanks for your contribution to our discussion today."

Fast-forward to the end of the school year, when I had a rather eye-opening experience. The special-education teacher asked me to come down to her office. "These are our IEP (individual educational plan) files; I want you to see something. All of our special-ed students are required to come in here at the end of every day and put all of their work into a file in these two file cabinets. Your student, Bobby, does that every day because he is on an IEP. But down here in this bottom drawer is what I want you to see." She pulled out the drawer, and in the back was a file that she took out. In it were all of the Post-it notes that we teachers had been writing! We had really been getting some positive comments on his recorder!

We had gotten this young man to "say it for himself." As a result of him finally saying positive things about himself, to himself, his life began to change ever so gradually. Four years later, he graduated from that high school with a regular diploma. He went on to enroll in a body-and-fender course at the local community college. I still see him once in a while. He no longer needs Post-it notes to find the good in himself! He can tell me immediately 20 great things that he is doing in his life.

That is what we need to be doing for our children. Post-it notes may not be necessary in your home, but I think that you can use the mental picture of a recorder and make daily attempts to store some positive comments on your children's recorders! Put your mind to it and be your children's advocates in your own home. Create situations where they can say good things about themselves, to themselves, and then watch them grow in positive ways.

Remember, if you try one way and it doesn't seem to work, try another. It's an awesome title: PARENT. Don't take it lightly. You can be the jumping-off point for a lifetime of positive self-statements in your kids' heads.

Chapter 9

Rule Five: Send a Constant Message of LOVE

Love is not just something you say; it is something you do! My grandfather passed on an old saying to me that goes, "You can fake like you care but you can't fake being there." To send messages of love to your children, you must show up. Love is not a spectator sport. Most kids could probably not articulate it, but almost every kid spells "love" T-I-M-E. If you're not willing to give your children lots of your *time*, you might as well stop reading! *Every technique from this point on will require lots of your time.*

There is a fallacy loose in the world. Parents try to rationalize a lack of time for their children by saying, "We give *quality time* to our kids." Baloney! It is impossible to turn on quality time. We adults can't turn on quality time with each other and it is even more impossible to do it with our children. There is *TIME*, period!

But love *is* also something you say. Love is time, but love is also a language. The human phenomenon of language is something of a mystery, yet we are universally able to use it in a powerful manner. Humans in every different culture speak their own language. In France, people speak French. In China, people speak Chinese. In Mexico, people speak Spanish. In the United States, people predominantly speak English. You can even identify different regions of the same country by the accent people use. "Y'all c'mon back and see us!" can only come from someone from the South, while "Paak your caa!" just as easily identifies a person from the Northeast. Ending a sentence with "Eh," identifies someone as being from North Dakota, Wisconsin, or even someplace in Canada!

Language is not genetically determined. Take a French child and raise her in a Japanese home, and she will speak Japanese. Raise a Japanese child in a Chinese home, and he will speak Chinese. Raise American twins in a Japanese home, and they will both speak Japanese. Separate them at birth and raise one in Japan and one in Mexico, and you will find two kids that look identical, but one speaks Japanese and the other speaks Spanish. *We speak the language that we are* exposed *to.* Language is a learned behavior. We learn the language we hear!

I will propose to you that *love is a language.* If we are not exposed to it, we will not speak it! Twenty-nine years in American public schools taught me that many kids do not speak the language of love. I found that telling a child of 15 that you care about him, that what he does matters to you, is often not understood: The child does not speak that language. I might as well have told the child something in a foreign language—it is just as difficult for the child to understand.

We learn a language by exposure to it. If we hear it spoken daily, we begin to speak it. Love is a language that must be learned in the same way: We must be exposed to it. If we ever expect our children to know that we love them, we must expose them to the language of love. They must hear the language regularly in order to understand it. Kids learn more from our back side than they do from our front side ... they learn more from what we do than what we say. Kids will imitate what we do more than they'll do what we tell them.

A Lesson in Diversity

Kids who are never told they are loved will have a terrible time trying to respect diversity or people of other cultures and nationalities.

Siblings who are never told that they are loved will have a very hard time loving each other. Kids who are seldom told that they are loved will find it very difficult to form lasting, loving relationships as adults, just as certainly as adults raised in France will have a difficult time learning English. Languages may be learned later in life, but it's well known that children learn languages much more quickly and easily than adults. Children who doubt that he or she is loved have a difficult time respecting diversity. They have never seen their own differences celebrated in a loving manner in their home.

In the classrooms where I taught during my last 14 years, we had many Hispanic students. In those communities, there was often open racial hostility, most of which had its roots in the fact that the kids from the two clashing cultures could never seem to empathize with each other. Empathy is a real part of love. It is part of the language! When you love someone, you feel empathy for the suffering and the happiness of the other. I witnessed many situations where kids would fail miserably at feeling or showing empathy for each other.

At one of these high schools, I received a real education in this very issue, and it was pretty graphic. On my first day on the job, we met with all of the staff at the school. The kids weren't due until the next day. We divided the faculty into two large groups and went into of the largest rooms in the school to discuss a couple of key problems we would be facing in the upcoming year. I was new to the school so I was hesitant to participate in the discussion. My group was to discuss what we were going to do about the escalating gang problem in the upcoming year.

Before this school year, the federal government had informed the district that we could not continue to operate two high schools of unequal racial makeup, one having more than 50 percent minority students and one having more than 50 percent white students. We were directed to integrate the two schools or else face federal intervention or loss of funding. This meant that my school was going to have to welcome in many more of the Hispanic population. The plan was to do it with recruiting and "magnet programs" that draw kids to unique opportunities the schools are offering. My school was offering new classes in English as a second language to draw the Hispanic student population to our school.

So there we were, discussing how we could be proactive in preventing gang activity among the kids who were going to be coming to our school.

One of the first comments was, "We have to take a strong stand against gang dress. We must ban gang dress at Eisenhower!"

I found myself agreeing with that statement, initially, because I didn't much like gang dress and was opposed to allowing it at school. My eyes were opened by the next statement from a member of our fine counseling staff, who said, "Well, if we're going to be fair and equitable about gang dress, we better own up to the fact that one of the most violent gangs in Yakima is the Cowboys! If we outlaw saggy-baggy, khaki, Dickie pants and certain colors of T-shirts as gang dress, then we better outlaw cowboy boots, Wrangler jeans, belts with big silver buckles, vests, and cowboy hats!"

Now, a common activity on Friday and Saturday nights was for a group of Cowboys to get together, arm themselves with baseball bats and clubs, and go out cruising in pickup trucks in the surrounding orchards. Any time they would come upon a lone Hispanic, they would stop and beat him up, or at least threaten to, and steal his money. (Many of the orchard workers are illegal aliens paid in cash under the table, which puts them in a dangerous situation: They carry large amounts of cash since they cannot put their money in a bank, and they also cannot report being robbed to the police because of their illegal status.) The Cowboys were a pretty violent group and in reality were probably responsible for as much violence as the drug gangs, but they weren't recognized as being as organized or dangerous, perhaps because their clothing was more acceptable to adults.

In fact, I was sitting there wearing the gang dress of the Cowboys! Almost all of my life I've worn cowboy boots and Wrangler jeans. I wear one of three big cowboy buckles and I wear Western shirts. All of a sudden, banning gang dress meant something different to me. I began to empathize with the kids. I realized what it would be like to be told that the way I dress is not acceptable at my school. I would feel like I couldn't be me. I realized that I dress with a sense of pride and self-identification, as do the kids we are dictating to. I realized that the reasons I dress as I do are almost exactly the reasons those kids have. I wear things that I have picked out because they are like my dad and Buck Minor, two of my heroes. The buckles I wear all have great significance to me and identify me with my family. Our students are just doing the same thing.

I also realized that if a dress code prohibited me from wearing the clothes I had on, I really didn't have any other clothes to wear! I would have to go out and get new clothes. I knew that if I had to, I could afford it, but that wasn't the case for the kids I taught. Most of them did not have enough money to buy a new set of clothes. If we told them that they could not come to school in the clothes they were wearing, most would have to choose between coming to school in their underwear or not coming at all.

Boy, was this an eye-opening experience for me. It forced me to really evaluate the real problem with gangs. The problem was not the clothes—and changing the clothes wouldn't change gang behavior at all. The problem was the illegal behavior of drugs, violence, coercion, and intimidation. It even occurred to me that a dress code seemed to be using gang tactics ourselves; we were just requiring different clothes!

Then I realized that I was a leader of one of the biggest "gangs" in the school: the football team. We had our "gang dress" we put on every Friday night. Then we would go to neighboring town to try to whip up on their gang. We even had our dress that we wore to school in the form of T-shirts and letter jackets. On game days, we even dictated that every member of our gang had to wear his game jersey to school! It suddenly occurred to me that it might be exciting if we could get those gangs to exist for excellence rather than drugs and violence. What if we could get gangs to stand for drug-free living like our football team? What if there were standards for minimum grades that had to be maintained for the kids to join the gangs?

I would never have been able to understand these students had I not known the language of love. If I had never experienced compassion, empathy, respect, or love, I would never have understood the motivation for the behavior of *many* of the kids I taught! The experience of those feelings allowed me to teach many kids whom I would never have been able to reach otherwise.

How Do You Say "I Love You"?

Simply put, we must teach our children the language of love by speaking it to them! How do we do that? By remembering this: Kids spell "love" T-I-M-E! Therefore, parents must give their time freely and lovingly!

My mother, Betsy Bledsoe, taught me about the power of love and taught me to laugh. She gave me my wings and is still the source of my strong roots. Do you think your children would say the same things about you? Can you define the things you've taught your children? If not, how might you structure your techniques to ensure your children actually use the lessons you're teaching?

We have put together here 10 ways to send a message of love to a child—or any person, for that matter. We would be foolish to say that this is a complete list of the methods of expressing love. It is not. There are many, many other ways, but these are a good place to start.

1. Say it.
2. Write it.
3. Make it.
4. Play it.
5. Look at them.
6. Listen to them.
7. Touch them.
8. Keep it positive.
9. Define it.
10. Teach it.

Say It

Kids should hear us saying "I love you" to them! It should be the first thing they hear every morning and the last thing they hear every night. They should hear it in the middle or at the end of arguments, on the phone, and at unexpected times. No matter what, you must say the words "I love you!" If you don't say the words, it's likely that all your other attempts at expressing love will fail. Without the words, your kids just might miss the message completely!

I learned this lesson in a very graphic way while coaching football in Benton City, Washington. As I was growing up, I had developed an idea that ruled my world until I was 36 years old: the idea that my father did not love me. Remember, earlier I said that it doesn't matter if an idea was right or wrong. This idea was wrong, but it didn't matter. It was in my head, and it ruled my world. It got there in an understandable way: Dad never said the three key words to me. He never said, "I love you," and so I missed all the other ways he said it to me.

Let me explain how I identified this terribly mistaken idea living in my head.

When I arrived at my job as head football coach in Benton City, one of the first questions the principal asked me was if I wanted to continue the school's tradition at homecoming. I told her I generally loved traditions, as long as they didn't have to do with hazing or put-downs. She described the tradition to me and it sounded cool. I helped

her, the vice principal, and the rest of the faculty plan the ceremony—
but I didn't expect it to be as wonderful as it was!

*My father, Stu, is pictured here with his four grandsons, our son Adam (lower left);
Lincoln Banks, my sister Janet's son (lower right); Beau Bledsoe, my brother Michael's
son (upper left); and our son Drew (upper right). Dad taught me to expect excellence of
myself, to dare to attempt big things, and that you cannot assume your children know
you love them—you must tell them. Are you waiting to tell your children you love
them? Are you telling them in many ways every day?*

Homecoming night, I met our team a full half-hour before our
usual warm-up time and we prepared for the game. Then, a half-hour
before the start of the game, we assembled under the goalposts for the
ceremony. All of a sudden, all the lights in the stadium were turned
out. Being a very dark night, it was impossible to see anything. Then
the players began to shout, "There it is!" About a mile from the field,
across the Yakima River, was a mountain in the Horse Heaven Hills.
On the mountainside, there is a huge "B," 20 or 30 feet tall, made of
rocks. As was the tradition, some students had gone up the mountain

and poured diesel oil on the rocks. When they saw the lights go out in the stadium down on the floor of the valley, they threw matches on the rocks—and now the "B" was engulfed in flame. From where we stood we saw a huge, flaming "B"! It was so cool.

Then, from the top of the press box above the stands, a spotlight beamed down between the goalposts where the team was gathered. The public-address system clicked on, and the vice principal began to introduce the seniors. As each young man was introduced, he stepped into the spotlight wearing his striking royal blue uniform … but he was not alone. As each boy stepped into the spotlight, his father joined him, wearing the boy's white traveling jersey with the same number. As the vice principal spoke of the young man's accomplishments, father and son would run under the goalposts to the sideline, followed by the spotlight, where they would meet the boy's mother. Each player would give his mom a rose and a hug, then they would walk to the middle of the field and stand as a family.

In this way, all the senior players were introduced and honored. Unfortunately, it wasn't possible for each boy to have both his mom and his dad in attendance, but we coaches had made sure that each boy had an adult male and an adult female who loved him to serve as his family. One young man had lost his mother to cancer four years before. His aunt gladly represented his mom in the ceremony. Another boy had been living in his car a few months before. When he was introduced, the pastor of the Baptist church wore his jersey and ran to the sidelines with him. When they arrived at the sideline, his English teacher met them. True, they weren't his parents, but they were adults who loved and cared for him.

This was a very emotional ceremony, and as I stood in the darkness watching, an idea occurred to me. I thought, "You know, Bledsoe, you missed a real opportunity here. You should have gotten all the coaches together and had all our parents here to be introduced with each of us. You missed a chance for all your team to see that, even as adults, we have families that are really important in our lives!"

But then that idea that had ruled my world for 36 years flashed through my head. I said to myself, "Well, that might have been nice to have invited my parents, but since Dad doesn't love me—after all, he never said those three magic words, 'I love you,' to me—it's probably best I didn't invite them. Yeah, it would have been cool to have Mom here, but not Dad."

Now, I admired my dad. In most ways I lived my life so as to imitate him. But he had never said "I love you" to me, and I had grown to believe that he really did not love me. He had grown up in a generation in which men didn't say stuff like that. It had formed an idea in my head, and that idea ruled my world—even as a grown man!

Standing there in the dark that night was a pivotal moment in my life, I whipped out my pen and my little notebook and wrote a simple note to myself, "Theme—Homecoming—Family." Next year, I was going to make "Family" the theme for homecoming week.

When homecoming week rolled around the next year, I called the team together at the end of Monday practice and said, "Guys, the theme for this week is Family. Are our families important to us as a team?"

Man, there was a long pause. Finally, one young man volunteered, "Coach, I know what you want to hear, but I also know you don't want us to just say what you want to hear, so I'm going to tell you like it is. I don't think that family is very important!"

"Wow, could you explain why?" I asked.

"Yeah," he said, "it's easy: Nothing will ever be good enough for my dad!"

"Go on," I pushed further.

"I will never please my dad. Back in junior high, the rule said that in order to turn out for football a student had to pass five out of six subjects. My dad said I had to pass all six. So I went to work and earned passing grades in all six subjects before he would let me turn out for football. The next year, that wasn't good enough. Dad said that

I had to get a C average in all six of my classes! So I went to work and earned a C average. And coach, *you* know what I had to do to turn out for football this fall: I had to make the honor roll last spring in order for Dad to let me turn out. Again I went to work and got a 3.0, a B average. I made the honor roll so my dad would let me turn out for football. This fall do you know what my dad told me? 'If you can get B's, you can get A's!' Right now, I'm grounded because on my mid-term report card, I had three A's and three B's. I'm grounded for grades I couldn't even get three years ago! I don't know what Dad will want if I get all A's ... I guess he'll want me to be the teacher or something."

Another player raised his hand and volunteered, "I know exactly what you mean. Last week I played the best game of my life, and I thought I would finally get some positive recognition from my dad. He came down to the field and walked straight up to me. I was thinking he was coming to congratulate me on the fine win, but he walked up to me, shook his finger in my face, and said, 'Why did you jump offside in the third quarter?' The only thing my dad could see in the game was the one mistake I made."

Then another young man joined in and said, "You guys know my dad. He's the town drunk, and he tells me if I ever drink, he'll kill me. He can't even run his own life and he's on my case!"

Well, this was not going the way I'd hoped! I'd been planning on having the team call to mind some meaningful, positive memories of their parents and families, so that when Friday's ceremony came around, they would have some positive memories in their minds as they were met by their folks. Unfortunately, this was going in the exact opposite direction!

Tuesday's discussion was more of the same, and I began to think more and more about how to turn the conversation in a more positive direction. When Wednesday rolled around, I said, "Would you mind hearing some observations from a guy who's a little farther down the line and has had a little bit more experience in life than you?" In hopes of making my point clear to them, I'd been thinking about the topic for three solid days. I had given a great deal of thought to what the kids had said about their parents and compared it to what my dad had said—or didn't say—to me. What they said sounded very familiar. It began to dawn on me that my dad *did* love me, but he had simply expressed it in demands for excellence and high standards of personal conduct. I saw that the parents of my football players loved their kids, and I could see them struggling, just like my dad had, to express their love with demands and expectations.

"Many times," I continued, "when someone loves you and sends you a message of that love, it doesn't feel much like love. For example, when I was growing up, our dad was like many of your dads. He pushed on me, my older brother, and my two sisters unmercifully. He demanded excellence from us and wouldn't settle for anything less. Sometimes he was almost brutal, demanding that we give our best at everything. Man, it didn't feel like he loved us at those times. He would say, 'If the Good Lord has dealt you aces, I'll be damned if you will come to my table and play deuces! Play the hand you've been dealt. If you are given the hand of excellence, you will not be average!' And boy, he could make it pretty uncomfortable for us if we ever slacked off.

"I remember the year I came home with a D in English. I tried to set the report card in front of Dad and get out of the room before he saw it. I wasn't that lucky. 'Hey, hey, hey!' he shouted. 'What is this? Is this D the best you can do?'

"'Well, yes, of course it is, Dad. You know I always give my best.'

"'Like hell it is,' he shouted. 'English is the language we speak in this family! You can do better than that!'

"I was sent to my room like a little child, to work on improving my effort.

"At the time it seemed that the *last thing* Dad was saying with those high standards was that he loved us, but guys, that's often how it is. The ones who really love us are the ones who demand the most of us! When someone loves you, they see goodness and excellence in you that others might never see. The ones who love us have the highest standards for us and demand that we give our best."

I tried to think of some other ways from my own background to explain what a message of love can feel like. "Another way that Dad sent a message of love to us kids was in the way he dressed. At the time, I simply thought he was on a mission to embarrass us! He couldn't seem to wear jeans unless they had holes in them and this was before ripped jeans were fashionable! He couldn't wear a pair of boots unless they were worn and covered with manure—preferably fresh! My gosh, you could always seem to smell him at the school open house. Then there was that old tweed coat he always wore. I was in sixth grade the first time I remember seeing it, and he was still wearing it at the awards banquet at the end of my senior year!

"Guys, I couldn't see it at the time, but those old jeans, those dirty old boots, and that old tweed coat—*they were all messages of love.* I just could not receive them at the time. You see, while Dad was wearing those old boots, I had new ones to wear, and so did my brother and my sisters. We also had stylish shoes of our choice to wear to school. And I had new football shoes, new basketball shoes, new track shoes, and all of the other athletic gear that I wanted. I couldn't see it at the time, but while Dad was wearing those ripped jeans, I had new ones to wear. So did my brother, and my sisters had new dresses in the latest styles. And while Dad wore that old coat, we kids had new coats each year. He wore the old one and bought new ones for us!"

Looking now at the young players on my football team, I said, "Pay attention, kids. Your parents are sending messages of love to you all the time as they make sacrifices for you. Remember to be aware and appreciative of the love that others feel for you."

Then it was Friday night. The "B" was burning on the hill and the lights were out in the stadium, and we were again ready to play the big homecoming game, all warmed up a half-hour before game-time. Just as the previous year, the vice principal began to introduce the seniors from between the goalposts. There I was, the old coach, standing on the sidelines and watching the ceremony. Again I was talking to myself, listening to the ideas that ruled my world. However, this night, I had a new idea going through my head. "You know, Bledsoe, I don't know if any of the athletes on this team learned anything this week, but you sure did! You learned that Dad was sending you messages of love almost every day of your life, and you just weren't listening. If any person in this stadium should have his dad here to be introduced with him as a significant part of his success, it's you!"

Well, I didn't have too much time to think about all this. It was soon game-time and I had a team to coach. That night our team was playing outstanding football and we were ahead by three or four touchdowns in the fourth quarter. We called time-out and began to substitute for the seniors one at a time. The crowd gave them each a standing ovation as they ran off the field, victors in their last home game.

As the game resumed for the final minutes, I felt kind of blue. Every year at this time, I would suddenly realize that this was the last time I would get to coach this great group of young men who were like sons to me. I was standing all alone at the end of the team box, thinking of how much I was going to miss each one of them, when all of a sudden, I felt an arm around my shoulders.

I turned and looked—*and there was my dad!*

That was another thing Mom and Dad had always done: They always showed up! Many times Dad didn't seem pleased by what he saw in my performance or actions, but he was always there … and here he was at this homecoming game, standing next to me at a tough moment for me, with his arm on my shoulder.

"Wow, Dad I didn't know you were here. How did you happen to be here?"

"Oh, your mom and I were in Yakima," Dad replied, "and I read in the paper that your team was playing its homecoming game, so we thought we would come and watch your team play."

"Wow, were you here for the ceremony at the start of the game?" I asked.

"Yeah, that was really a neat ceremony, son," he offered.

"Gee, I wish I'd known you were here—I would have liked to have had you and Mom introduced with me."

I could hear distinct disappointment in Dad's voice when he said, "Yeah, I would have liked that, too, son."

Trying to make it up to him, I said, "Well, why don't you come in the locker room with me after the game? I'd like you to meet my team."

"I'd like that," he replied.

So following the game, Mom rode home with Barbara, and Dad came into the locker room with me. I didn't even need to introduce him. The guys were great to him, shaking his hand and introducing themselves. Shoot, some even hugged him. It was the first time I ever saw my dad give someone a 'high five,' and it was a fun time. Then the guys were off to the homecoming dance and Dad was helping me pick up the uniforms and the towels in the locker room … and I wanted to say something to my dad about my newfound understanding of his love for me, but I chickened out again and didn't say anything.

Then, about halfway home, I stopped the car. There, on a country road outside of Benton City, I finally got up my nerve and said, "Dad, those kids were really neat to you tonight."

"Yes, they were, son. I don't think I've ever felt so welcome as I did with your team tonight. Those sure are wonderful young men. You have done a masterful job of coaching them."

"Well, Dad, it wasn't exactly an accident that they greeted you so warmly. You see, sir, I've been talking to them about 'my dad' all week long. Those young men were friendly and warm to you tonight because they heard some pretty neat stuff about you.

"Dad, I know that this will not square the ledger with you, but I'm going to make a start right now. I know I've been an ungrateful son for years. I've been telling my team about events that I should have been telling you 'thank you' for all of my life … but I haven't, so I'm going to try to do that right now.

"Dad, I need to thank you for demanding excellence of me—often at times when I could not find excellence in myself! Thanks for pushing on me, demanding that I give my best. Dad, it was because of your pushing that I was able to coach that football team tonight! When I was growing up, I just couldn't see what a wonderful gift you gave me when you demanded excellence, but this week I realized that you did it because you loved me."

"Sir, another thing I need to thank you for are those old jeans, old boots, and that old tweed jacket you used to wear. I now know that those were a real message of love to us kids, because all the time you were wearing those old clothes, we had new ones to wear. And not only did we have lots of nice clothes, we had a roof over our heads, food on the table, money in our pockets, and gas to put in our cars. You constantly went without, so that we kids could have, and I want to say thank you for that, Dad.

"I also want to thank you for teaching me to appreciate my freedom and to never take it for granted."

There were about 20 other things that I needed to thank my dad for, many very personal, and I will never forget that evening as long as I live. After I thanked my dad for more of those wonderful things, he looked over at me. He had tears in his eyes. I think it was the first time I had ever seen my dad cry. He had a way with words, and I will never forget the words he said that evening! "Kid, you are the sun that lights my day and the moon that lights my night!"

And then I heard the magic words I had been longing to hear all my life. Dad looked at me through his tears and said, "I love you, son!"

Then he reached over and grabbed hold of me and hugged me to him. Dad was a strong man and he could hug hard! While he was hugging me, I heard those magic words three more times, "I love you, I love you, I love you!" The first time my dad was able to say the words "I love you" to me was the time I was able to say "thank you" to him!

Now, there are some important lessons in this little story. The first one is pretty obvious: We all need to say "thank you" to the people who care about us and show they care by their actions. We all need to appreciate the many ways people show their love.

However, the really important lesson for parents is that we must say the words "I love you" to our kids! "I love you" must be the first thing our kids hear in the morning and the last thing they hear before they go to sleep at night, and they must hear those words repeatedly all day long! We cannot assume that our kids know that we love them simply because we raise them and sacrifice for them and have high expectations of them. We cannot wait for them to grow up, as I did, and then finally understand. *My dad failed to tell me that he loved me, and, therefore, I missed all the wonderful ways in which he* showed *me he loved me!*

This is not a risk we can take. We cannot risk any misunderstanding when it comes to love: We must say the words! Once we have done that, we can focus on the other ways to communicate our love to our children. If we fail to tell them regularly that we unconditionally love them, they may miss the message when we send it in other critical ways. If we say it first, they will understand that the other messages we send—concerns, expectations, disappointments—are *also* messages of love. My dad told me that he loved me in every other way, but because he did not say the words, I missed the message.

I have two more significant observations to offer from this event with my dad. The first is that it is never too late to say "I love you"! My dad waited until I was 36 and he was 58 to say those words to me, but it meant the whole world to me when he finally did. He only lived six more years, but I never saw him again without his telling me that he loved me. Those were six of the best years of my life and certainly the best years of my relationship with my dad.

The second is that it would have been a real crime if my amazing and loving father had gone to his grave without ever hearing the words "thank you" from his son! It is never too late for that, either. Many people have told me that, after hearing that story about my dad and me, they finally realized what had been missing between them and their parents. Hearing that story motivated them to build some emotional bridges of their own. If you're one of those people, let me encourage you to take the necessary action to build a relationship with your parents. Take it from me: It is well worth the effort.

Write It

Writing is a magic form of human communication. There are a number of tangible reasons that writing is a wonderful, unique, and effective method of communicating.

First, what you write to someone is more permanent. It delivers your message today, tomorrow, next year, even 10 years from now. If you write something to someone, it will last as long as they keep it. If you would like to have a degree of immortality with your children, and with future generations, just write to your kids. Write often, write from the heart, and be sure to touch on many subjects. When you write to kids, it doesn't have to be mushy or lovey-dovey. Write about things that are important to you, like ethical and moral issues that you feel are important, or values and spiritual issues that are close to your heart.

Our grandfather, Albert McQueen "Mac" Bledsoe was a great example of this. He used to write regularly to all 11 grandchildren— and it seems, in retrospect, he was a little devious in his methods. He would write letters, but in the margins he would write little sayings. It now seems as though he wrote those letters just so he would have an excuse to fill the margins with thoughts and ideas that he felt we would need in life. He would write little things like, "Never trust a man who is always well dressed!" Later, he took me aside and told me what he meant by that particular pearl of wisdom. He said, "Young man, I'm not telling you to distrust well-dressed people. The controlling word in that sentence is *always*. If a man is *always* well dressed, he's either a phony or he is not doing much! If a man is really doing something of significance, he is occasionally going to get a little sweaty and roll up his sleeves, get a little dirt on his hands, or grass stains on his knees." When you stop and think about that little gem, there's a lot of truth in it.

In the margin of another letter, he wrote, "Nobody can make you feel inferior without your consent." Now, I have discovered that Granddad was not the original author of that bit of wisdom (he was often pretty careless about citing his sources)—Eleanor Roosevelt is given credit for that statement. Granddad was on the opposite side of the political spectrum from that great lady, but he still thought it was a bit of wisdom I should have, so he wrote it down and sent it to me.

He shared so many wonderful ideas with us kids that he has directed my actions for years, even though he is no longer alive. He is immortal because I still read his teachings daily and they are still some of the critical ideas that rule my world. I am amazed now to think that, at about age 10, I began to write down Granddad's sayings. I still have most of them. My only regret is that I didn't save his letters so I would have his wisdom in his scrawly old handwriting.

To show the power of writing, one need only go to the book _Make the Right Call_, co-written by our son Drew and an important author, David Brown (www.positivelyforkids.com). In that book, Drew thought that Granddad's sayings were significant enough to put one at the bottom of each page. Now, there are literally hundreds of thousands of kids and families benefiting from Granddad's habit of writing down key ideas for his grandkids!

Some very important things happen when you write to your kids. Writing is magic: It says you thought about your kids while you were not with them. Do you think about unimportant people when they are not around? Writing says that you think about your kids often. Write them often, even if it's brief and spontaneous. Many times the best form of writing is on pieces of paper that tell your kids where you were when you wrote. Pick up a piece of wrapping paper that identifies itself as being from work and write on the back of it. Tear off a piece of cardboard from a welding rod carton and write on a clean space on it. Write on office stationery, write on envelopes, write on the back of discarded invoice copies. Write notes and put them in their lunchboxes.

Write notes and letters and put them in their clothing drawers to be discovered at unexpected times. Write notes on bathroom mirrors in lipstick! Make picture albums and write captions under and around the pictures. In doing that, you will direct their memories of past events. Barbara put collages of pictures on our kids' walls. She wrote captions all over the pictures. Sometimes she would use the captions to get our kids to say things for themselves. For example, I remember one picture she staged. She had Drew take Adam over to the window and show him a bird's nest in the tree outside his window. As Drew was bending down pointing at the nest with his hand on Adam's shoulder, she took a picture. The next week I saw the picture on Drew's newly made poster. It had a caption under it that read, "You are so patient with your little brother!" Every night when Drew would go to bed, he would look at his poster and read the captions. By making those posters, Barbara was structuring Drew's self-talk. At that time, his little brother was really annoying Drew, but Barbara was getting him to alter that by having him recall a vivid picture of his being patient with his brother. It worked! You can probably think of many pictures you have of your kids where you could stimulate positive self-talk by adding captions describing the picture in a positive manner.

Write letters to your children and mail them to them. Let them go to the mailbox and find a letter from you with a postmark on it. The postmark is proof that you have gone to the trouble of actually mailing it. Sure, they live in your house, but a letter is unique and important. It will get their attention in a way that a talk in the kitchen simply won't! A letter says, "This is something that I want you to know with some formality."

When you write, you can word your thoughts and ideas very carefully and precisely, before it "gets all over the kids." Everyone has had the experience of saying something you didn't really mean in the heat of the moment. Writing prevents that; when you write, you can do it over until you get it just right. One of the most loving things parents can do for their children is to write to them about what they believe: about honesty, integrity, compassion, courage, love, family, and so on. Write down your precise spiritual beliefs. Write to your children about your beliefs about freedom, America, and democracy. Write about what your family means to you. Write down bits of wisdom about various aspects of life, to help your kids make big decisions. Give those writings to your kids on a regular basis.

You can even write poetry for your kids. I said this to a class of parents we were working with in Walla Walla one night, and a big dad in the back of the room raised his hand and said, "That's fine for you, Bledsoe, you're an English teacher. But I can't write poetry! I quit school in the eighth grade, and I'm a welder for a living. I can't write poetry!"

I thought for a second and decided to risk a little personal information. "Sir," I said, "the only class I was ever kicked out of in high school was English! I don't have a degree in English—I just teach it! But here's a little tip for you on writing poetry to your kids, if you're willing to accept it. Get a little notebook or piece of paper and a pen. Then go down to the Hallmark card shop. Their cards are even categorized by occasion for you. Spend a little time there and read the cards until you find one that sort of says what you want to say ... then get out your pen and paper and copy it down!"

"You can do that?" he replied in a rather loud voice.

"Well, I don't know if it's legal, but I've been down there a few times and I've never been arrested by the Plagiarism Police! But if you're worried about copyright law, buy the card and give the author his due, then go out to your pickup and copy it down. I guarantee what will happen. You'll start writing the author's words and you'll say, 'I wouldn't say it quite like that,' and you'll change it into words more to your liking. And I'll guarantee you something else. You'll get to the end of the author's words and you won't feel like you're finished; you'll have a rhythm going and you'll write another verse or two."

No writer has ever had a totally original thought. Every writer gets inspiration somewhere, so take a risk and write nicely to fit special occasions.

When you write to your kids, it becomes permanent. It says the same thing today, that it says tomorrow, that it says next week, that it says next year, that is says 10 years from now. What you write will say the same thing as long as the writing is kept. We can ensure that our kids keep the writing we give them by modeling for them what we do with things that have been written to us, especially things written by them. Let them see that when we receive special cards, we keep them in a special place. Let them see that we occasionally go back to those cards and read them. Help them select a place where they keep special written messages—a locking box, leather-bound notebook, or scrapbook.

If you have written to your children about important ideas over an extended period of time, your ideas will have a much greater chance of becoming the ideas that rule the world of your kids.

When you write to your kids, don't just write about them or even *to* them. Just write about ideas that you feel are important. Write down what you feel about freedom, pride, happiness, loyalty, honesty, diligence, family, and other topics of significance. Don't write as if you're telling your kids what to think. Tell your kids that these are important ideas to you and that you simply want them to know what you think about them. I have essays my dad wrote about free enterprise, capitalism, democracy, freedom, and many topics important to him. I have read and reread them. Dad died 12 years ago, but I hear him speaking to me each time I read one of his writings.

Write to your kids! Write often, write well, and write from the heart.

Make It

Making something for a child is a great way to show her you love her. Make doll clothes or toy cars for your little ones. Dads can make furniture for dolls and moms can make stuff for cars. It doesn't have to be complicated; making simple things is often the best way to communicate your love!

On a particularly disappointing day in the life of a young one, make that child's favorite meal. It is easy to get things mixed up and make their favorite meal when something great just happened. We take our kids out to dinner following a home run or making the honor roll, but when something disappointing happens, we may desert our kids. With just a little bit of thought and care we can turn this around! Think about this: Your child comes home with a bad grade on a paper or had some other disappointment. Sensing that he's had a tough time, you prepare tacos, his favorite meal, for dinner. After dinner, you walk into his room and say, "Hey, looks like something went bad at school today. How about we see if we can find a solution to the problem. I love you, and no matter what, I'm on your side!"

The act of making his favorite meal is proof positive that you are not the enemy and that you are available to help. The food just might be the confirmation of love that the child needs to allow you to help!

You can also make tapes or CDs for them. When they're little ones, we can read their storybooks onto audio tapes for them to listen to while traveling or as they play in their rooms. (In doing this Barbara even put our kids into some of the stories.) We can sing songs onto tape for them. We can record them simply talking while they're young, then let them listen to their own words a few years later as a clear demonstration to them of how much they have grown, matured, and changed.

Videotape works great for this, too. Make videos of them playing or talking, then watch the videos together as they grow. Have a tape or CD playing in the background while you're taping, to remind them of their past taste in music. You might even use this as a way to influence their taste in music, by pairing music with pleasant experiences on video that they'll play over and over.

You can also make tapes or CDs of music for them to listen to while playing. We hear so many parents expressing frustration about the quality of music available for children. With just a little bit of effort, parents can influence the music our kids listen to by recording music that our kids like *and* meets with our own criterion of acceptability. Listen to your recordings in the car or during playtime in the house or the yard.

Another key to making things as an act of love for our kids lies in making things *with* them. When they're young, we can make cakes with them or make cards with them. As they grow older, the things we make can suit their age and interests. A couple who are friends of ours adopted a daughter. As she grew up, the father began making a dollhouse with her. As she grew older, the dollhouse became progressively more sophisticated and more detailed as she directed the building and remodeling. Her dad got to build in his shop, which he enjoyed, and the daughter got to spend time with Dad in his shop. Dad and daughter would also visit stores looking for new furniture to build and new modifications to make in their house. Their shared dollhouse hobby lasted for years and years, into her early teens. It bonded father and daughter—it was meaningful, loving interaction that spanned time.

Collections can work in the same way. Collecting trading cards or little cars can allow a mom to interact with a young boy whose interests are in sports or cars without Mom having to play the game or get dirty working on motors. Parents can interact with their kids by adding to the collection and finding ways to store and categorize the items. Pay attention to your child's interests and let that guide what you collect. Beware of collections driven by television: Those are often artificially created interests, and the collections are very limited and driven by advertising campaigns that manipulate your kids for financial gain.

As your children grow older, match their age and changing interests. Keep your eyes and ears open, and you might be surprised at the amazing interactions that can spring up as you make something useful and educational!

One of our sons began bringing home magazines on radio-controlled models, which had been a childhood interest and fantasy of mine. He would go to bed and I would find myself sitting up reading his magazines! One night as I was reading I suddenly thought, "These new models are really cool." I hadn't had the money for them as a child, but now I had more money and the models were cheaper! So I encouraged my son to find out which models he liked best, then I went to the model shop and did some shopping.

One rainy Saturday I got him up early. He was reluctant to get up until he saw the radio-controlled monster truck kit. "Wow, whose is that?" he shouted.

"Ours!" I shouted back. We had the greatest weekend playing and building the model. After assembling the truck, painting and applying the decals over about eight hours, we were finally ready to run the machine ... then I found out that he had no intention of letting me run it! He did all of the driving and I was feeling cheated—so I went out and bought one for myself. We built that one together, too. Then we staged races! I received an ongoing education as we played together with the models. There was a whole world of add-on options for these cars, which created an ongoing relationship as we modified and tweaked our models. We built road racers, dirt-track racers, and motorcycles. We spent hours running to and from the model shops, shopping for parts and updates, and building and racing and running the models we built. It was a blast. It gave me an excuse to return to my childhood and explore something I had been fascinated by but unable to explore. It gave my son a great outlet for his interests, and above all it represented years of shared time and shared fun. During those hours of shared time, we built a relationship that transcended models!

One day I went to the dentist and the technician recognized me as "the guy who teaches parenting classes," so she asked me, "I have a 14-year-old son who's getting interested in cars, and I was wondering what you would think about me buying a car for us to restore?"

My reply was, "What a great idea! You will never be sorry that you did it!"

Every six months when I went in for my cleaning, the technician would give me an update on the car and the mother/son relationship. It was really something to marvel at. They bought a 1965 Ford Mustang, took the body off the frame, and began a complete restoration from the frame up. They finished it just in time for the son to drive when he got his driver's license at age 16. She told me he was so protective of their carefully restored project that she was completely certain he would drive carefully.

I continued to be amazed at what I heard over the next couple years. This car became a bonding agent between mother and son. They would go to swap meets together to look for parts. They would attend "hot-rod runs" with other Mustang owners. They went all the way to Las Vegas to attend Hot August Nights and hang out with other hot-rod enthusiasts! They spent hours together, sharing their common interest.

So we've learned that moms can build cars and dads can build dollhouses! The key here is relationship building. It takes time, but it's extremely meaningful time, and it's fun! Think carefully and ask yourself where you might find a common interest with your children. One of the keys to developing shared interests is to start early. I doubt if the dental technician would have found that her son was as interested in restoring a Mustang with his mom if she had waited until he already had a driver's license!

The conversation that springs from a common interest isn't forced, it's natural and spontaneous, and so is resulting relationship. The dental technician said that she had the greatest conversations with her son while working on their car. One night she was lying under the car with her son, attempting to put in the transmission, when her son looked over and asked her, "Mom, when I'm on a date with a girl, is it okay to …?" and he asked her a very personal question. He would never have asked if they hadn't had the relationship built around the car. Under their car was the place he felt relaxed enough to ask the question.

As you're building with your children and for your children, you will build relationships.

Play It

Seek opportunities to play with your children. That is what people do when they love each other: They play! All too often we find parents who take the job of parenting too seriously. They seem to think that every conversation has to be loaded with guidance and advice. That's not true. Play and laughter is a great way to build a relationship with a child. It's also a great way to extend our own childhood! Let your hair down and play with your kids, if for no other reason than to have some fun.

I learned way too late in life that adults can buy water balloons, too. Imagine this: You leave work early some sunny afternoon. You fill up 30 water balloons, and you have them in a bucket on the roof, where you hide, waiting for the school bus to drop the kids off at the corner. As the kids unload, you start launching your ammo at them. (Did you know that from that height, you can get about six in the air before the first ones land?) By the time the projectiles begin to hit, you're again out of sight. The kids are dodging and trying to find out where the water balloons are coming from. Then one kid spots you on the roof when you emerge to continue the bombardment. I guarantee you not one kid will say, "Your dad is so dumb!" They will say, "Your dad is so cool! My dad would *never* throw water balloons at us from the roof—let's go get him!"

My gosh, sometimes dinner can wait—especially if it's snowing! In the life of an eight-year-old, snow is exciting and fun, and you'll probably find it's fun for parents, too. Turn off the stove and go make a snowman! Dinner can wait. As a matter of fact, a late dinner might also be fun for the whole family. Eat by candlelight in front of the fire after coming in from building snowmen.

Don't wait until your kids say that there is nothing to do in your hometown and then try to argue with them … you will lose that argument. Have an activity planned for your family every weekend. Go on a picnic. Play a game in the yard. Play simple card games before dinner. Play Cribbage, Gin, or Go Fish and keep score over weeks and months. Play for a penny a point or a dime a game. It will be a reason to continue playing. (You can even lose on purpose to bait the game into "extra innings.") Play tricks on your kids, and let it be known that you are fair game for tricks as well. Short sheet their beds, put surprise toys in their shoes, put blocks of wood in their sandwiches, and get ready for some fun tricks to be played on you. (It might be necessary to establish some rules and guidelines, though.) Don't be surprised if you try to get up from Thanksgiving dinner and find that someone has been under the table and tied your shoelaces together.

In all the shared laughter, you'll find that play is magic for building lasting relationships. Remember that the people we laugh with are usually the people we seek out in times of difficulty. If you have built a tradition of laughter with your kids, they'll feel much more comfortable coming to you in times of need or trouble.

Hang in here with me in the next few paragraphs. A few years ago I read that wonderful book *Men Are from Mars, Women Are from Venus,* and it had a profound effect on me. What the book says to men is pretty simple. In 20 ways the book exhorts men to give a woman what she wants! When I read that, I decided to try the advice at home. I studied Barbara and tried to determine what she really wanted, and that year for Christmas, I decided to give her what she wanted!

On Christmas morning, she received her gift. It was in front of the house in the back of my pickup: $600 worth of vertical grain, all-clear, 1×4-inch, tongue-and-groove redwood. No, I hadn't messed things up like you might think. You see, what I found out, after considerable thought and investigation, was that what my wife wanted more than anything else was to remodel the bathroom in our house! Because it was impossible to remodel the bathroom without her knowing, what I had done for her Christmas present was to make her a card describing exactly how I would do the remodeling job and bought the wood to panel all of the walls of the bathroom.

I was right on with the gift. I don't think I've ever seen my wife that excited with a Christmas gift! In the card, I promised that by our anniversary, June 10, I would have the additional $1,000 saved up to buy what we needed to complete the remodel job. There were still a few little problems: We needed a new toilet, sink, and bathtub. You see, they were all blue, but not the same color of blue. And then there was the problem of the tile around the tub. It was in good repair, but it was pink with a black border. (The colors would never have bothered me, but they were driving Barbara crazy.)

When June 10 finally rolled around, I waited until the boys were in bed and then asked Barbara if she would sit down at the dinner table with me. I had saved up the money like I had promised, and I had gone to the bank and gotten the thousand dollars in small bills. I spread the money on the table. Then I asked her to hold my hand and look into my eyes, because I was going to ask her a very important question. I let the suspense build for a moment and then hit her with the question: "What do you think our boys will remember most when they are our age—a new toilet, tub, and sink … or a water-ski trip to Dworshak Reservoir?"

Thank God for the wonderful woman I married. She put off her dream remodel job, and that summer we took a weeklong camping and water-skiing trip with the money!

By the following Christmas, I had again saved up the money, and that time I sat her down and asked her, "What do you think our kids will remember most when they are our age—a new toilet, tub, and sink … or a ski trip to Snowbird, Utah?"

That winter we went skiing in Utah with the remodel money. Then the next summer we used the money for a family trip to Disneyland and Sea World. Shoot, we had money left over to go down to Rosa Rita Beach in Mexico and eat lobsters on the beach!

The point is that when our kids were growing up, we threw caution and money to the wind and simply played with them! Ask either of our kids today what was the color of the toilet, tub, and sink in our bathroom in Walla Walla and they couldn't tell you. But they could tell you about the trips we took! They could describe in detail playing cards and games in a tent while we waited out a storm during our camping trip to Dworshak Reservoir. They could tell you about the motel where we stayed in Twin Falls, Idaho, on the way to Snowbird, and how we laughed when the door kept blowing open during the night. They could tell you about the magic trip to Disneyland—and how Disneyland was the *low-light* of the trip!

I sincerely believe that kids will be much more secure and capable of making big decisions for themselves if parents simply play more. If parents drove older cars, lived in smaller and less pretentious homes, had fewer fancy and expensive toys, and spent more time playing with their kids, kids will be more secure in their belief that they are important, valued people. If parents played more games with their kids, they might not find it so difficult to talk with their kids about important things, because they will have built comfortable relationships with their kids through years of play and laughter!

Parents, let your hair down and play with your kids. It's an excuse to enjoy life and be young forever! And in the process, it's a chance to build a fun and lasting bond with your kids.

Look at Them

Look at your children and let them know that you love them by that look. We all know the unspoken delight of catching someone looking at us and knowing that person loves us. Let your kids feel that glow of affection often.

Go to the school play or church Christmas pageant and let your child catch you looking at him while he stands to the side in a critical scene in which he has no speaking part. Let your kid catch you watching her on the bench while the winning basket is being scored at the other end of the floor. Let your child catch you watching him in the parade while everyone else is watching the float in front of the band. It will be clear, unspoken proof to your children that you came to watch *them*—not the play, the game, or the parade!

Let your kids see themselves just the way that you see them. Take the video camera along and take pictures of them just the way that you see them. Zoom in on your kid right when the critical scene is taking place on the stage so that all that can be seen is your child! That's the way you see him, so let him see it on the tape. Take pictures of your children on the bench during critical moments in the competition. That will let them know that you are watching them with a love that transcends winning or losing silly games. Zoom in with your video or camera as the band marches by and let them see that you are not watching the band or the floats; you are watching them!

Caution might rule here, and your knowledge of your children should guide you. Some kids might be sensitive about being filmed while on the bench or on the sidelines. Consult them, but at the same time tell them what you did and why you did it. Tell them that it often takes much more courage to be on the sideline and be positive than it does to play the game. Use the videotape as a way to tell your kid you're proud of her team spirit and her support of her team. This could be an entree to a whole discussion of what it means to be a team player.

The fact that your child might be embarrassed by the movie of him sitting on the bench should not necessarily cause you to avoid shooting the tape, but it might tell you what audience to show it to! Those tapes might be reserved for viewing by only the two of you. When you shoot those videos, be careful to make them positive experiences. Give your child feedback on the reasons you're proud of her action.

Remember also that the video camera has a microphone on it! Make some loving comments to your kids while shooting. It's like allowing your kids to overhear you saying nice things about them to others. The only thing to remember is that your comments are permanent and will definitely be repeated. Be careful what you say!

What you tell your kids by being there and watching them is, "No matter what is happening around you, I am watching you because I love you!"

Listen to Them

Stop what you are doing. Right now, stop what you are doing and *listen to your children*. Resist the urge to say it for them. Resist the urge to jump in and criticize or even to formulate that "yes, but ..." in your head. Democracy teaches self-worth because one of the basic tenets of democracy is that all must participate for it to work! Another tenet of democracy is that every person must have the chance to be heard. Your children deserve to be heard. Our children cannot be heard if we are always talking! Push things aside and give your kids your undivided attention. Stop mixing ingredients in the kitchen. Turn off the TV. Put down the paper. Turn away from your desk, look them in the eye, and *listen!*

Parents are constantly telling us that their kids won't talk to them. In almost every case, the problem is not that the kids don't want to talk. The problem is that the parents don't want to listen. Kids learn quickly. All it takes is "Can't you see I'm busy!" or "Not now, I'm reading the paper." If you never listen, don't be surprised if in time your kids never talk to you.

As a schoolteacher, I did some of my best teaching in the moments between classes or during the quiet time in the mornings before school and in the afternoons after school. Kids would drop by to talk. Notice that I didn't say they stopped by to listen! That's a key distinction. I learned some very good "listening words" from a counselor, and I have used them for years. There are six of them: "Oh!" "Really!" "Wow!" "Uummm!" "I didn't know you felt like that!" and "Tell me more!" While the kids would talk, I would fill in pauses with one of those six words or phrases that let kids know we hear what they're saying. Those words and phrases encourage the speaker to continue, but they offer nothing approving or disapproving.

It blew me away when I found out how powerful it was to simply listen. Kids would drop by and spend 20 minutes describing a problem, dropping the most shocking information about their lives right in my lap. As often as not, I helped them more by just listening than I ever could have by offering advice. As they talked their way through the problem, they would work out their own very logical solution. All they needed was a listening ear and a caring heart. After talking they would get up and leave, saying, "Mr. Bledsoe, you're the greatest. You always give the best advice!" All I had said were those six words and phrases. They solved their own problem.

Isn't that your goal for your children? To have them solving their own problems and making their own decisions? Well, your listening gives kids a chance to work out their decisions before they act. If they know you will listen, they can work their way through a tough decision by trying out their ideas on you first.

We've finally learned that listening is often all kids want from us. We started asking, "Do you want advice or do you just want me to listen?" Nine times out of ten, all they want is for us to listen. So bite holes in your tongue and listen!

People who love you will listen to you. If you love someone you will listen to them, so listen to your children. You love them!

Touch Them

Sometimes a hug is the only way to reach another human being. Always have one available for your kids. Little ones need to be hugged often. It will fix a world of hurt for them. As they get older, children may become uncomfortable with public shows of family affection, but don't let that fool you into thinking they don't want to be hugged. It might be a good idea to stop hugging them right in front of the middle school, but a hug when they get home is still okay. They may be saying, "Not now!" but don't stop hugging them.

A pat on the back may be worth a thousand words of praise. Walking by a youngster working on a drawing or writing a thank you letter and stopping just long enough to pat her on the head or on the back is often all the reward she'll need to keep on with the productive behavior. That touch of approval can convey so much, so take the time to reach out and do it.

It is certainly okay to hold a child's hand during a touching or frightening portion of a movie. I think I learned that it was okay to feel strong emotions when my mother took me to see *Bambi* as a child. I was feeling a lump in my throat during a particularly moving point in the movie when I felt the reassurance of my mom's hand reaching over to hold mine. Her touch said, "I understand," far better than any words could have at that critical moment. It said, "I recognize that this touches your heart, and your feelings are normal." She didn't understand exactly what she was teaching, and I didn't understand exactly what I was learning, but her touch accomplished both!

When you reassure your children with touch at critical times in their lives, it will come back to you 10 times over. Many times some pivotal episodes in life can teach us more than one lesson. I wrote in an earlier chapter about just such an experience for me. John Matau, my best friend of 33 years, died after a 5-year bout with cancer. His death changed my life in a number of ways.

I was afraid of faltering in delivering the eulogy at the service honoring John. Falling to pieces in front of everyone would not be the way to honor John. As I said earlier, I worked out a signal with the clergyman conducting the service. If I didn't think I could muster the courage, I would just give him the sign, and he would read my prepared eulogy. Well, the service was under way, and I was just about to give him the sign—I was sure that I was going to make a mess of things—when suddenly I felt the grip of big, strong hands on each of my arms. It was our two sons, Drew and Adam, sitting on each side of me. I guess I never knew until that moment just how much strength a man can draw from the touch of a loved one. Their touch said, "You can do it, Dad," better than any words could have! As I walked up onto the platform, I felt the reassurance of my sons' strong hands as they accompanied me up to the podium. Each time I felt myself faltering, I felt the strength of those young men who were now my support and my strength. They seemed to know, at this critical moment, that the best thing they could do for their dad was offer the strength of their touch. They were right! I again learned how important it is to give children reassuring pats or hugs at critical times in life.

A pat on the back, an arm over the shoulder, or a hug can often be the only way to express love. Use them all. When kids say, "Don't hug me," most likely they just mean, "Not in front of my friends!" So hug them later, but don't stop hugging them!

Keep It Positive

In the world today it seems that the loudest people get all the attention. I'm not suggesting that we parents start shouting and being obnoxious, but I am suggesting that we speak up! We shouldn't let people with negative outlooks win just because they are the only ones expressing themselves. If you have a positive thought or a positive outlook on some issue in your household or your community, you must have the courage to stand up and be heard!

When it is written in your local paper that there is a terrible "movement" taking place at the local middle school because some graffiti had to be removed, speak up and point out that there were 1,342 kids in the school who did not paint anything on the walls of the school!

Write letters to the editor of your local paper to celebrate the kids and families in your community who are doing good works. Don't operate in crisis-management mode and wait until someone else says something negative before you speak up. Develop a habit of always having something good to say, so that your kids always hear you talking about what is right rather than what is wrong. Instead of talking about the fact that now almost half of all marriages in America end in divorce, read aloud from the papers the reports of couples celebrating silver anniversaries! Point out people in church who have had perfect attendance for 11 years. Introduce your kids to firemen who have acted heroically and pulled kids from burning buildings. Be sure to allow your kids to see the people who plan and do the work to put on community events like the fair or the banquet at the school. Don't allow yourself to be critical of those who have done lots of extra work to make an event a success but left out something you would have done; let your kids hear you talking about all the things that went right with the event!

The ideas in your kids' heads will rule their world. Remember that! You may think you're talking about how things ought to be, but often, the idea kids pick up on is that everything is wrong and nothing is right. If you spend time talking about what's wrong with the world, the "wrong" is winning! Talk about what is right!

That is how wrong ideas work. Somebody does something hurtful or hateful and then we read about it, talk about it, and the wrong idea begins to occupy our thinking. We must take control of that in our homes. We need to talk about good things and positive ideas! We shouldn't be surprised if our kids have a negative outlook on life if all they hear is their parents talking about how bad things are at work and how nobody ever does anything right. If you want your kids to have a positive outlook, you need to talk about good and uplifting things with your children!

Make a bulletin board at your house dedicated to local heroes. Clip out articles from the paper about good things happening in town. Always have ideas for fun things to do on the calendar in the kitchen. Clip out articles about upcoming concerts and live theater, then go to them. Invite a local hero to dinner. Head on down to the skateboard park and watch the kids show their stuff. Join the walk for the food bank. Join a Habitat for Humanity building project. Clean out some closets for Goodwill. Take a meal over to a shut-in elderly couple and bring some joy into their life. Take a Christmas dinner to a needy family the week before Christmas.

The biggest tragedy in all the negative on TV is that it is the only voice in the room. Talk back to the TV. Turn it off and talk about something happy or uplifting.

If you want your kids to see the good side of human nature, you must show it to them! Don't think that you can just sit back and wait for the world to bring a positive outlook to their door ... because the world won't do it. You must stand up and create their positive outlook for them. Sound off to your kids about what you believe and why you believe it.

Define It

Mom, Dad, home, family, friend, honesty, LOVE. Your *actions* will define these and many more words in the lives of your children. What are your actions saying? Your children's definition of "Mom" and "Dad" will forever and always be what you are and what you do. Ask yourself, "How do I want my kids to define *family?*" Then let your actions define it that way! Your kids won't remember much of what you say, but they will remember forever exactly how you acted!

Let's take a look at the word *family*. What do you want the definition of family to be? Whatever happens in your home will forever be the definition of family for your kids. Are you living that definition? If not, your kids will have in their heads what you are living and not what you want them to have. If what happens in your house is arguing and shouting, then their definition of family will be just that! Do you want your kids to view a family as a place where you can bring difficulties and failures? Then you must let your kids bring those things home to you! You cannot just harp on the negative things and expect your kids to place high value on family!

I suggest that every family sit down and write the definitions of some key words: *family, mom, dad, honesty, togetherness, happiness, security, love,* and so on. After you write the definitions, ask everyone, "How can we live out those definitions?"

Let's say you all choose respect as a critical aspect of being a family. How would you live out respect? Would that mean that everyone in the family is listened to? Would that mean that some members of the family are allowed to be a little bit different from the others? In what ways? Would it be okay to have different tastes in music? Would it be okay for some members of the family to use foul language, or would that be something that the family might take a hard line on not allowing? How about "put-down humor"? Would that be allowed or would that be another activity the family might take a firm stand against?

Speak out! Let kids see the cup is more than half-full even when the media seems to be presenting a different picture. You might even find that this exercise of finding the positives in life changes your outlook as well.

Let your kids see you giving an extra thank you or an extra tip to an especially cheerful waitress or service technician at the auto shop. Write thank you letters to unsung heroes in your community and ask your kids to sign them along with you.

We can sit and curse the darkness or we can light a candle—it's up to us. Many times when we light a candle we see that others are doing the same thing. Model positive action for your children.

Teach It

Give your children this list! Actively teach them how to be loving to family, friends, grandparents, people less fortunate, their parents, or their pets! Continually look for opportunities to model love for your children.

Teach them that if they want to have a friend, they must *be* a friend. Start them off at age two telling their friends that they care for them (say it!). Help your kids make cards for each other; as they get older, have them write their own cards (write it!). Help kids develop habits of games and activities with other kids and grandparents (play it!). Help kids make things with other kids and make things for others (make it!). Teach children of all ages to ask questions—and then listen to the answers (listen to them!). Show your kids how to hug others at times of need or times of hurt (touch them!). Teach your children to speak up for good things that they see in others (keep it positive!). And finally, teach your children to teach others to do all of the above (teach it!).

Your children will lead fulfilled lives if they develop behaviors and habits that connect them to others in loving and caring ways. By teaching your children these steps, you will be preparing them for some amazing happiness. If your children go out into the world able to care for and express caring to others, it might not much matter what they do for a living because they will live fulfilled and meaningful lives!

The time they most need to hear the message is the time you feel least able to send it!

When you are at the point of tearing your hair out—or worse—that's probably the time when your children most need to receive your message of love. In the heat of a conflict, it can be hard to remember that *you are the adult*. Be the adult in every situation: Rise above the anger and express your love for them. This is not permissiveness. You can still be very strong in your expectations for your kids' behavior. You are simply confirming that you love them, unconditionally, regardless of their actions. Fill their hearts with your love at this moment when it is most open to receive love, and it will be so much easier to ask for desired behavior.

Taking Action

1. Write each of your children's names on each day of the next week on your personal calendar. (A day-planner would work great if you use one.) Look back at the 10 ways to tell your kids you love them and write one way after each child's names on each day of the week.

2. For the next week, follow your plan and communicate your love to your children once each day just as you planned! Do not do this for any other reason than because you do love them. Be careful not to expect or anticipate any specific reaction on their part. Just send your messages of love to each of your children each day. It takes fewer than five minutes.

3. Take notes on your actions and your children's reactions, and any other observations you have as you go through this process for a week. Remember to record both positive and negative actions, reactions, and observations.

Showing We Care

Here is a list of ways we can show our love for our children (and remember that spouses can benefit from the same loving actions!):

1. Notice them. Get caught staring at them—even throw in a wink.
2. Listen to and answer their questions with your full attention.
3. Kneel, squat, or sit so that you are at their eye level.
4. Create traditions and fight for them.
5. Laugh at their jokes.
6. Include them in your jokes. (If that makes you uncomfortable, maybe you ought to change the jokes you tell.)
7. Smile a lot.
8. Acknowledge them with a heartfelt "Good morning!" and a "Hi!" each time you see them.
9. Discuss their dreams (nightmares included).
10. Be relaxed in their presence. Just hang out with them.
11. Say their names.
12. Contribute to their collections.
13. Hide surprises for them to find.
14. Go and find them at unexpected times.
15. Play outside together.
16. Surprise them.
17. Remember their birthdays and other significant days in their lives. ("This was the day you took your first step!")
18. Ask them about themselves.
19. When they ask your advice, give them options.
20. When you ask questions, listen to their answers.
21. Stay with them when they're afraid.
22. Tell them you miss them when they're not around.
23. Follow them when they lead.
24. Play with them—adults can start water-balloon fights, too!
25. Expect their best ... and accept that it is not perfection.

26. Be available.
27. Do what they like to do.
28. Share their excitement.
29. Be honest.
30. Be sincere.
31. Include them in conversations.
32. Brag about them when they don't think you know they are listening.
33. Call them from work.
34. Eat meals together.
35. Plan discussion topics for dinner and announce them ahead of time.
36. Tell them your expectations for their behavior.
37. Practice the behaviors with them before they are in the situation.
38. Introduce them to adults and tell the adult something of significance about them.
39. Help to see mistakes as learning opportunities and not failures.
40. Record messages to them.
41. Record them talking.
42. Videotape them just being themselves, like during one of those dinner conversations.
43. Write them letters and send them in the mail.
44. Go places together; take them along on errands.
45. Build something together.
46. Give them jobs at home that require thought and planning.
47. Welcome their suggestions and use them.
48. Make decisions together.
49. When you make decisions, include them in your thinking.
50. Help them take stands on moral and ethical issues, and then stand with them.
51. Hug them.

continues

continued

52. Set boundaries, but help them to understand the reasons for them.
53. Believe what they say.
54. Tackle new tasks together.
55. Cheer for their accomplishments.
56. Encourage them to help others, and recognize them when they do.
57. Create a safe environment for them.
58. Share secrets.
59. Laugh.
60. Stop and enjoy time together, even a minute at the bathroom sink.
61. Be consistent but flexible.
62. Praise loudly, criticize softly.
63. Let them act their age.
64. Tell them about yourself.
65. Tell them what you believe and why you believe it.
66. Help them become an expert at something.
67. Laugh.
68. Ask their opinion about things.
69. Show that you're excited to see them.
70. Let them tell you how they feel.
71. Display their artwork around the house—nicely framed!
72. Thank them!
73. Smile at them constantly.
74. Keep promises, even small ones. In their eyes, they're all the same size.
75. Laugh.
76. Find a common interest.
77. Let them pick the music and listen to it with them.
78. Apologize when you've done something wrong.

79. Hold hands.

80. Take a walk.

81. Read aloud together.

82. Read moral literature (like the Bible, or the Koran, or books on ethics) and help them understand it.

83. Use your ears more than your mouth.

84. Show up at events.

85. Learn from them and let them know what you learned.

86. Tell them how terrific they are.

87. Always suggest a better behavior when they have chosen an inappropriate one.

88. Laugh.

89. Be nice.

90. Look them in the eye when you talk to them.

91. Give them space when they need it.

92. Use time in the car for interaction.

93. Tell them how much you like being with them.

94. Develop a "secret word" for your family.

95. Meet their friends.

96. Meet their friends' parents.

97. Admit it when you make a mistake.

98. Be honest.

99. Give them a private nickname and don't use it in front of others. (Let them do the same with you.)

100. *Above all, laugh, Laugh, LAUGH, and laugh some more.*

Chapter 10

Teaching Your Values to Your Children

Values are complex ideas like honesty, integrity, respect, diligence, spirituality. Values, when well taught, become the all-encompassing ideas that rule the world of your kids and cause them to make good decisions for themselves. Values usually require extensive definition, clarification, and illustration by you, and then again by kids as they internalize them into their minds and their reality as principles for making choices about behavior, actions, friends—everything! Your values are the most important ideas that you share with your kids, so you should teach them with the most care. Remember that you haven't taught children something until they use it as a principle for guiding their own behavior.

A child of eight who has practiced honesty since age three and has a good working definition of honesty will be much more likely to be honest when it might seem easier to stretch the truth or tell an outright lie. Let's say that your eight-year-old's teacher has just confronted him about being tardy at school. Now, your child has a decision to make. Does he tell the teacher the truth, that he was goofing off in the park on the way to school, and accept the consequences of missing noon recess for five days? Or does he fudge a little bit and say that his little brother was scared on the way to school, so he detoured to escort him to his preschool and that's why he was late?

He might reason that other kids do this and get away with it. He might reason that it didn't really hurt anything; he got to school a little bit late, but he didn't miss anything that can't be made up. Or he might just think that nobody will ever check, he won't get caught, and it seems like an easy way to dodge a harsh punishment.

Or he might have a pretty clear definition in his head about how to handle situations like this: "Say what you mean, mean what you say, and do what you say you're going to do!" He may have had similar situations at home where he could have lied and gotten away with something, but instead he told the truth and got positive feedback from you that he did the right thing. He may have read stories about kids who told the truth and were rewarded for their honesty. He may have been given opportunities to tell the truth when lying would have seemed easier, but you showed him how to weigh the situation and tell the truth. He also may have had situations at home where he saw the consequences of telling a lie and then finding that he was forced to tell *another* lie to cover the first, and maybe *another* lie to cover the second. When you caught him, you didn't ground, punish, or humiliate him but instead taught him the wisdom of telling the truth the next time, and then gave him the chance to correct his lying by reenacting the event the right way!

So what will your child tell his teacher? If he has experienced the positive outcomes of telling the truth and has that idea well developed in his head, he'll be more likely to tell the truth and accept the immediate negative consequences. He'll know that in spite of the unpleasantness of missing recess, in the long run he'll feel better for having owned up to the truth and knowing that his word is good in the eyes of his teacher. He knows it because you taught it.

As you teach your values to your children, keep Rule 4 in mind: "What they say to themselves is what counts!" To teach your values to your children, you must use methods and techniques that get your children to say it for themselves. You can tell your children that they should be honest until you are blue in the face, but it will not influence their behavior until they adopt honesty into their personal ideas about themselves. You are trying to put these important ideas into their heads so that they will use them to make the big decisions in their own lives—so that they become the ideas that will rule their worlds.

Be careful while attempting to build positive ideas in your child's head, that you watch carefully to see if your positive statements are being stored as such. Look for telltale signs that your children aren't repeating it as you said it. Look for obvious signs, like "Oh no I'm not!" or "You always say that!" phrases muttered under the breath.

It would be nice if raising kids was always an exact science, but it simply isn't. I wish I could remove the ambiguity or confusion, but it would be foolish to pretend I could. One thing I will offer at this point is something I've said a couple times earlier in this book: *You must spend lots of time with your kids!* The outgrowth of spending lots of time with your children is that you get to know them very well. The better you know your kids, the easier it becomes to read their reactions to the guidance you give them. Teaching values to children is a complex process. Anyone who attempts to tell you different is misleading you.

An Example to Follow

If you believe that "Honesty is the best policy," you should make sure that your children hear it often and hear it expressed in a variety of ways. They need to see honesty bring good things to you and to themselves. They need to have many experiences where they have the opportunity to tell the truth to see that the truth is always the safe way to go. They need to see famous people being honest and using honesty as a guiding principle in their lives. Kids also need to meet local heroes and role models who use honesty as one of the principles guiding their lives.

In today's society, like in the past, kids have heroes. This is a good thing. Allowing children to have heroes is a great way to reinforce ideas and values you want them to use in guiding their lives. However, it seems the process of selecting heroes in modern society has become muddled or confused.

Fame by itself shouldn't make a person a hero. Barbara and I have experienced this from both sides: first as parents of two sons who had their own heroes while growing up, and now with two sons who have distinguished themselves as outstanding athletes and are often themselves the objects of hero worship.

Now, we do believe that our sons are worthy heroes. They're both moral, admirable men with a strong sense of family. But it's alarming to see how so many people have selected them as heroes without knowing much about them. Many children have been taught to or at least allowed to select their heroes/role models based on nothing more than skill at a game or fame; few of these kids know much about their heroes beyond that. If children were taught some criteria or standards for selecting role models, it might be different.

Allow me to illustrate with a personal example. Barbara's father, Dick Matthews, died suddenly last year. His five grandchildren delivered the eulogy at the funeral. It was obvious to all in attendance that Grandpa Dick was a hero to all five. As they spoke of him through their tears, they all mentioned his hero status in their eyes and used words like loyal, dedicated, hard-working, honest—a man whose word was his bond—as well as describing a fun grandpa who always had a smile a mile wide.

Dick Matthews was quite a fellow. Few men could outwork him outside the home. Dick built houses for a living but he also ran a farm and did odd jobs on the side as was needed for extra money. If necessary, I'm certain he would have taken a night job to provide for his family, and he did all of his work cheerfully, with a sense of purpose and a bounce in his step. Inside the home, it was a different story. In his house, Dick was the king and Maxine, his loving wife of 46 years, waited upon him hand and foot. It was not a "modern" romance, but one from a previous generation, and it worked beautifully for them. Dick earned a living, and Maxine kept up the home.

Ten years ago, tragedy struck that loving couple when Maxine was severely weakened by a terrible stroke. From that instant, she has needed around-the-clock care rather than being the family caregiver. Without the slightest hesitation, Dick became her 24-hour-a-day, 7-day-a-week caregiver. On top of that, he began to do all of the housework! He did all the laundry, cooking, cleaning, shopping, and everything else Maxine had done for all the years in their partnership of love.

A year ago, while out to breakfast alone with Dick, I was struck by the enormity of the change he had made on behalf of his loving wife. I asked him how he had made such an amazing change so suddenly and so cheerfully. His answer really affected me that day, and it will always be in my memory. He looked back at me, got tears in his eyes, and then quietly said, "One day 46 years ago, I said 'I do.'"

At his funeral, each of his grandkids said that one thing they had learned from Grandpa Dick was to honor commitments. They each got the message. They saw it repeated every time they were with Grandpa Dick and Grandma Maxine.

As parents, you need to help your kids select people like Dick Matthews as heroes. We all know people in our families and neighborhoods who are worthy of being heroes to our kids because they live by the ideas we want our kids to live by. We must not be so careless as to think that kids will seek out these remarkable but often quiet people; we need to teach them what characteristics define a hero. In pointing out these people in the immediate community, kids receive real-life reinforcement and repetition of ideas we want them to adopt as the ideas that rule their world. Sure, an athlete makes a flashy hero, and many are worthy of the status, but be careful to teach your kids what makes a person *really* worthy of hero or role model status.

The Top Twenty List

I would like to propose a concrete procedure that you can use to guide your children to adopt the values they will use in making the big decisions in their lives. I can personally attest that this process works: I was taught to use it as a kid and have in turn taught it to many kids. Hopefully it will help you, too!

When I was in junior high, our YMCA leader Alden Esping had us go through this process and it had a profound effect upon my life. I was in eighth grade, and I made up my list of the "Top 20 Things I Want to DO, BE, or HAVE in My Life." The amazing result of having made this list—which I still have, by the way—is that I had accomplished 17 of the things I had written by the time I was 23! And I had accomplished all 20 by the time I was 33! I accomplished every single one of the biggest dreams I could dream in junior high. Every one!

As we were making our lists, Alden was careful to guide us in the selection of the items we chose for our lists. He said that we could select things like honesty, friendship, loyalty, and other values for our lists. We had a ton of fun with Alden, but we always spent time in serious discussion of critical issues. As we took trips together or camped out, he continually brought up topics dealing with values. Do the same with your children.

Encourage your kids to keep their list a secret (I'll explain why a little later). Mine is a secret, too, but for the sake of demonstration I will share just a couple things I put on my list and how having those on my list changed my life.

The number-one thing on my list was to play football for the University of Washington Huskies. Okay, maybe that's pretty shallow, but it's what I dreamed of at that point in my life! At number five on my list, I put being drug-free. There's a critical connection: I met my first drug-pusher in the strangest of places—in the training room at the University of Washington! My list had helped me to make that team, and suddenly I was confronted with a trainer offering me steroids as a way to get bigger. I turned him down, because just that morning I had looked at my Top 20 List and seen my commitment to be drug-free. It was easy to make the decision because I had made it long ago and re-affirmed it every day since! My answer to the trainer was, "Thanks anyway, but I'll make the team without drugs or I won't make it! Drugs will not be a part of my training."

My grandfather, Vice Admiral Albert McQueen (Mac) Bledsoe is at the far left. He taught me the importance of writing down life's important lessons, and in so doing ensured that I retained them. Alden Esping is at the extreme right in this picture; he taught us how to dream big dreams and work to make those dreams come true. Are you making sure your children spend lots of time with people like this?

A friend of mine was in the training-room with me that day, and he didn't have a list to look at. He hadn't made a decision about drugs, so what the trainer said sounded pretty good. He went ahead and used the drugs. We both made the team, and he got bigger with the steroids, but he was probably sterile from about the third dose he took. And now he is dead. Doctors are pretty sure he was killed by complications associated with abuse of steroids back when he was in college.

My list saved me and allowed me to enjoy a full life. Not only that, having a Top 20 List allowed me to preserve one of the most important things for my future—something I hadn't even considered to be in danger at the time: having kids. Now on my list, my kids are number one! If I hadn't had my list of the ideas I had chosen to rule my world, I would be an entirely different person today. My life wouldn't be nearly as full and exciting as it is, because neither Adam nor Drew would be blessing my days! My list allowed me to make a critical decision with lasting, positive results for my family and me.

Would you like your child to have positive ideas ruling his world, guiding his decisions at those critical times? If so, read on.

Step One: Considering the Possibilities

Buy or, better yet, make a notebook for your children to use as a place to record their investigation into the world of possibilities for their lives. The earlier in their life that you do this, the better. Five years old is not too young. You might have to write in it for them at age five, but as soon as they can write, let them take over.

And 18 is not too late! Kids of any age can benefit from this process. I am active with Parenting with Dignity in many prisons across America, and I hear an interesting comment from almost every prison that teaches this process. For many inmates, this is the first time that they have actually identified, analyzed, and *chosen* the thoughts that they have in their head—and experienced the power of taking control of their own destiny. Prison officials talk about how "criminal thinking" brings about criminal behavior, but it does no good to condemn criminal thinking without teaching how to replace it with Top 20 thinking! Once inmates realize that their thoughts are their own, they develop their own goals, and their behavior changes as they direct themselves toward their goals. Program your mind with positive ideas and you will get positive behavior!

Many parents find that the best way to present this notebook is with some ceremony, like a rite of passage. Take your child to dinner with you, alone. (If he has siblings, get a sitter—this is his night!) Dress up and go to a nice place. Present the notebook as a gift after dinner. The goal is to establish in your child's mind that this notebook and the process it represents are really important.

As you present the notebook to your child, you might say something like, "You are rapidly arriving at an age when you're capable of making some of the big and important decisions in your life. I want to help you to begin to carefully select some of the ideas that will rule your world. This notebook will be a place where you can keep a record of the work that you are going to do. I hope that this evening will be the starting point of a happy, fulfilled, and self-directed life. I am doing this with you because I love you."

Tell your child that this is a place to start a list of everything they can DO, BE, or HAVE. The next day, or sometime very soon after you present the notebook when you both have time to spend on it, start the list by filling at least two pages with possibilities. Be ready with a variety of possibilities. Your suggestions will set the stage for all of the following listing that your child will do. Suggest that they can BE a carpenter, a friend, a doctor, happy, a musician, and on and on. They can HAVE money, self-pride, a 1959 Chevrolet, nice clothes, respect, and a happy family. And there are infinite things that they can DO. They can swim, ski, design bridges, laugh, and draw.

Then keep the list handy and add to it at every possible opportunity. If you have one of these discussions on the way to school in the morning, suggest that they take out the list and write down the new possibility. Keep the list available while you travel, which often opens the eyes to possibilities. Encourage your kids to always be on the look out for new possibilities and add to their list at any opportunity. Make mental notes and write them down later, but help your children to become *possibility-thinkers*. (You might find some interesting possibilities for yourself in the process!) Help them to see that all around them are possibilities for them to DO, BE, and HAVE! Make sure they know that you are there to help them choose wisely but that this selection process must be their choice.

As you drive past a road crew, just say, "There you go, you could be a flagger in a construction crew." As you pass an accident, point out to your kids, "You could be an EMT, a policeman, or drive a wrecker. Or you could design a better airbag!" As you drive through a big city, make comments as the ideas strike you, like, "Look at that, you could wash windows on a high-rise!" or "You could have an office on the hundredth floor of a tall building." Or "How would you like to run a restaurant, or maybe a soup kitchen for the homeless. Hey, you could even be a street-person and eat in soup kitchens!"

As you point out choices, be sure to continually show that making good decisions always involves ruling out a whole lot of bad decisions. Don't be afraid to let them list both positive and negative possibilities; in my suggestions there are some possibilities that I wouldn't want my children to choose for their list. By including some of those undesirable possibilities in your suggestions, you will show that it's acceptable for your kids to list some things that you might not want them to pursue and thus you can discuss the strengths and weaknesses. The goal is to get your children to *possibility-think*, to really investigate possibilities for their lives.

This period of possibility-thinking is a wonderful time for you to discuss the merits of the values that you would like your children to adopt as the guiding principles in their lives. You can give your child books that deal with some of the topics. Many of the books written for young kids deal with themes of honesty and loyalty. It might work well to read the book together and then discuss the theme of honesty as a possible item to include on their possibility list.

Many parents use possibility-thinking as a time to read the Bible or other religious materials to find more ideas to include on the list. When you see inappropriate or immoral behavior or criminal action (newspapers and television are great places to find examples), take the opportunity to discuss and apply your values, morals, and ethics to the situations. An article in the paper telling of six kids who vandalized a local hardware store is your cue to discuss respect for personal property and the law, and possible ways to make decisions about getting involved in such behavior. A TV sitcom can stimulate discussion on decisions involving interpersonal relationships.

Ask your kids to explain how the values you've been discussing could have changed the outcomes for the people in these situations.

Try to do as much listening as talking. Practice using the "listening words" proposed in Chapter 9. Try not to be judgmental. You are simply discussing. Let your kids know how you feel, but let your kids think out loud as well. While doing this, you're building a relationship that allows your children to think through decisions with you before they ever get in the tough situations. Slowly but surely, you find that you have discussed many of the values that you would like to have your kids adopt as ideas to rule their world. If there are values, morals, or ethics you would like to discuss, search out stories, books, articles, TV shows, or songs that deal with them and use them as discussion topics.

Use time in the car as you are driving to school, as you're eating dinner, as you're playing a board game with your kids for these discussions. With younger children, the question might sound like, "Last night we were watching *Todd and Copper*, and I was wondering what you thought about their friendship. Did you think that Copper was disloyal by obeying his master, or should he have refused because of his friendship with Todd?" With an older child who is reading *Romeo and Juliet*, you might ask, "When Romeo came sneaking into Juliet's yard, was it wrong for him to go against the feud between her family and his? After all, her father was his father's mortal enemy."

Or as you listen to some music, ask something like, "Do you think it's okay to sing about treating women with disrespect?" or "Do you think that songs glamorizing drug use are good to listen to?"

I must say it again; this process will take a considerable investment of your time with your kids. Once you develop the relationship with your kids where they feel comfortable having these discussions with you, then you will find that they start seeking your advice on many more. You now have a context for asking your kids if they have given consideration to the values you are discussing for inclusion on their list of possibilities.

Continue this process until your child has filled at least six pages with possibilities. There should be at least 300 possibilities on each page. (Three columns of 50 on each side.) If their possibility list does not contain that many, it does not really constitute a list of possibilities. To have only 200 to 400 on the list says that there has been considerable elimination and selection already going on. The selection process will come next! Once the list reaches six pages your child is ready for Step Two!

Step Two: Selecting the Top Twenty

From their 6-page list of possibilities, have your children pick the 20 they would most like to DO, BE, or HAVE in their life. If your child is five, the list might be pretty basic stuff, but don't worry: You're teaching an ongoing process. This list can and should be modified as life goes on!

As your child creates his or her Top 20 list, a very important transition takes place. Up until this point everything has been open for discussion because it is all in the context of possibility-thinking. Nobody is expecting action to be taken on any of the possibilities because they are just possibilities!

This next step is different. The Top 20 list is now destined for action. These ideas are being selected to rule the world of the children. At this point, the list must become the private property of your child! As the parent, you are now excluded from seeing the list.

In keeping this list private, you prevent this process from becoming an exercise in pleasing others rather than an exercise in self-guided behavior. I cannot tell you how important this element of privacy is. The list absolutely must not be shared with anyone, especially not you, the parent! Some families will use the Bible or other religious book as a guide in selecting items for this list. Others families will guide their children to seek the advice of others, like grandparents, pastors, counselors, or youth leaders in selecting their Top 20, but the list itself must be private. Children must be allowed to ask for advice, and then be free to ignore it if they disagree.

Another reason kids should keep their list a secret is that the people who are most likely to steal their dreams are the very ones who love them the most! Think about it. When was the last time you heard a mother in her front yard shouting, "Go for it, Billy! I know you can go higher in that tree! There are four more branches—go for it!" Well, Mom might be right to not encourage Billy to climb any higher, but overcautious parents often act the same way trying to get their children to be "realistic" in their goal setting. In the case of our oldest son, Drew, my first advice to him if he had told me in the eighth grade that he wanted to be a professional football player would have been to tell him to be reasonable. I would have tried to protect him by having him attempt something safer and more realistic!

No, parents will almost always have kids aim at safer, less risky goals, dreams, and governing ideas for their lives. Resist the urge to know what your kids are aiming for. Occupy your time with them helping them to see the strengths and weaknesses of items on their list of possibilities. Discuss the possibilities and leave the final Top 20 list to the child.

Many parents have a difficult time with this, but 29 years of experience slowly taught me that to teach kids to think for themselves, *we must let them do it!* Think about this for a minute. If you convince your kids that this process will positively work to bring about desired outcomes in their lives, and then you tell them that they have to show it to you, they will develop a list to show to you. And then they will have a real list for themselves that they keep private. Why not empower them to build their private list in the first place?

Have confidence. Your input comes into play during the formulation of the list of possibilities for the items on the list. Many parents feel that they are giving up too much control. That's the ultimate goal! Your goal is to raise an independent person capable of intelligently guiding his or her own life. You're trying to help them build a set of guidelines to use in making those huge decisions that they will be faced with when you are not present to decide for them.

Teach the values, morals, and ethics well as you are guiding them through the possibilities and let them pick. They will do it anyway. Go back to the start of this book and to the start of my education about raising children. Listen again to what Dr. Cobb said to us when Drew was born: "This child is not yours. He is just on loan to you for 18 years. He already has a will of his own." We must empower kids to use their will to make good choices for themselves. We must teach them how to do that and then have faith in their ability to use what we have taught them.

Once the child has picked a list of 20, have them prioritize the list from 1 to 20, starting with the one that they would most like to DO, BE, or HAVE. Tell them that this list is just a starting place, a work in progress, that they can alter it at any time. The list constitutes a road map for their life, and they can pick a different road at any time. One should always check the map to ensure that the road they're on will get them to the destination that they have chosen.

I have never met anyone who would walk into an airport and say, "I want a ticket!"

"Well, sir, where to?"

"Oh, it doesn't matter. I just want a ticket to go somewhere!"

Everyone wants to know where the plane is going, but it's amazing how many people are going like crazy with no idea of where they're headed! This process helps your kids have a direction. If you succeed in this exercise, you will have given your children a gift that few in the world have received. You will have blessed them with knowing where they are heading and with the peace of mind that comes with knowing that they have chosen the destination. Even though you do not see the list, it will give you great comfort to know that your kids are heading into life with a purpose!

Remember, it will be easier to convince them to do this if you also do it!

Step Three: Read It Three Times a Day

Guide your children to take time out of their day to read and think about their Top 20 List. One of the most powerful ways to guide their behavior is to model it for them by doing it, too. If religion is a big part of their life, some families will encourage their kids to include this list in their daily prayers. Praying makes more sense to kids if they have something specific to pray about. Put into a context of prayer, the list will often take on a much less self-serving and material feel or focus.

Explain to your children that there are two critical times each day to read this list:

1. **First thing in the morning.** Starting the day with a positive picture in mind of your top priorities will ensure that any opportunities to fulfill those goals and aspirations will be maximized—and anything that could detract from or derail those goals will be avoided. Reading the list first thing in the morning programs the mind to focus on the important events and opportunities during the day.

2. **Last thing at night.** Reading the list at the end of the day allows the mind to focus again, to affirm and assess your progress and success during the day. A review of your values and aspirations at the end of the day really allows you to confirm that the list is still worthy. Every time you review the list, the ideas on it become more powerful in ruling your world!

3. **A time they choose.** The child should select the third time. Guide your child to select a time when it's possible to focus and have private time. Some children do it the first thing when they arrive home from school. During weekends and vacations, a good time might be right after lunch or right before dinner. The earlier you start your kids, the easier it will be to establish a routine.

Most parents find that it is easier to establish time for focus and reflection if it is participated in by all members of the family. I receive comments from parents who report that it really helps them to focus on their goals for the family and their techniques for parenting. Athletes take time to exercise their muscles, and we train for jobs and skills in the workplace, so it stands to reason that taking time to focus on the important values we use to guide our life is also something that has value.

Most parents find that 10- to 15-minute periods for thought and discussion between work and the duties of home and family bring a focus and a calm to the family that they have never known.

Are vs. Ought to Be

I would like to mention something very critical to guiding kids to be self-sufficient, independent thinkers and decision makers. In order for them to have the confidence to make the big decisions in their lives, they must be treated as if they can. Telling them that they *ought* to be capable of something is very different from treating them as if they *are* capable!

Don't treat them as if they *ought to be* what you want them to be. Treat them as if they already *are!*

The ultimate insult to a child is to tell him that he "ought to be," because that sends the hidden message that "you are not."

Teaching kids that they are in charge of selecting the ideas that will rule their world and then getting right in the middle of the process and either doing it for them or showing them that they have chosen wrong teaches the opposite of what you set out to teach. Treat them as if they can and you will be surprised at how well they will do.

How many times during his career do you think people told Michael Jordan he ought to be a good basketball player? Probably never. He *was* a great basketball player; probably the best ever. If someone told him he ought to play better, he would have thought that this person thinks he's not as good as he could be.

How often do you think people told Mother Teresa she really ought to give more service to others in need? Again, the answer is probably never! She was one of the most humanitarian people in history. To have told her that she ought to give more would have implied that she wasn't giving enough.

Of course, standing at the top of their respective fields, Michael Jordan and Mother Teresa could instantly dismiss the criticisms of anyone who might say they "ought to be" better! Your children don't have that confidence and experience yet—and it's your job to give it to them! You must treat your children like they are capable of *anything*.

As you treat them as capable individuals, they will begin to display those capabilities. There is a huge difference between telling a kid that he never cleans his room and telling him that he ought to clean his room. There is an equally big difference between telling a kid that he ought to clean his room and treating him as if you expect him to clean his room.

What would you say to Michael Jordan if he played poorly? "Wow, Michael, I was really shocked when you let yourself throw up that bad shot!" After all, he's so great, it's a shock when he makes a mistake. If your son doesn't clean his room, you could express the same surprise that his performance doesn't match his abilities by saying something like, "Wow, Billy, it surprises me that you keep your clothes in a big pile in the middle of your bedroom. I would think you'd have them organized in your closet and drawers! You're so smart and organized, I just can't believe you haven't organized your room."

As you guide your kids to fill their heads with positive ideas of things they would like to DO, BE, or HAVE, you can augment their ability to perceive themselves as capable of accomplishing their dreams if you treat them as capable of doing things around the house. Give them big tasks to do around the house. After all, how would you treat a highly capable adult living in your home?

If you have a child in need of some skills in managing time, give him situations to manage time but teach him how to handle the job!

An Exercise for Life

I want you to see what I am trying to do with this whole book. This rite of passage of giving your children a notebook in which to record their values, goals, dreams, and aspirations is not just an exercise for one evening; it is an exercise for life. Don't view the discussions you have with your children about ideas to put on their list of possibilities as a one-time event—hopefully, the discussions with your kids will last a lifetime. Gradually, your children will rely less and less upon you, and more on their own judgment and the processes they've developed for critical thinking. Your guidance now will give them a basis upon which to make big decisions for a lifetime.

My experience should serve as an example of what I am trying to teach you to do with your kids. Alden Esping taught me a process for picking, evaluating, and prioritizing a list of values, aspirations, and dreams. I began with that process at 12 or 13, and I'm still involved in that process today. When I began, my list was very limited and basic—since I was young and lacked experience—but over time my list has grown in depth and scope. There are now 262 ideas that have been on my Top 20 list. I have crossed all of them off as accomplished except the ones that are in my current Top 20. This has been a lifetime exercise. I still value my relationship with Alden and still am in touch with him on a regular basis—but I don't need to seek his counsel often, because he taught me to think critically for myself.

As you work with your kids on building their skill for critically selecting the ideas that will rule their world, it would be good to go back to Chapter 5 regularly to ask yourself what you are trying to teach your children. That will make it easier to focus your efforts and select strategies with a prospect of success. Having had discussions about choices for life will also make it easier to have discussions about any immediate behavioral or disciplinary situations that come up.

It is so much easier to have these discussions about moral and ethical decisions with your own children if there are other children that they know who are being raised in a similar manner. In Chapter 13, I will discuss a plan you can use for creating a whole community of families who are challenging their children to lives based upon sound moral and ethical decision-making.

Thoughts to Remember

Here are some other thoughts that you might keep in the front of your mind as you are guiding your kids to make great decisions for themselves.

- **If we want to teach responsibility, we must give responsibility, not take it away.** When your children make mistakes and act irresponsibly, give them instruction in how to be responsible and give them tasks requiring responsibility.

- **If we want kids to feel important, we must treat them as if they are.** We must listen when they talk and ask questions. We must seek their advice on important family decisions and give them important jobs around the house.

- **If we as a society want our kids to grow up with a sense of belonging, we must offer a place to belong.** Our homes must become places where kids can bring their problems and find a listening ear. We must make our homes places where our children seek joy and happiness. We must make our homes into sources of information that can be used in making big decisions.

- **If we want kids to be intelligent, we must provide opportunities for them to think.** Our children need to be taught that thinking about values and moral and ethical decisions is a worthwhile activity. The only way we can teach them this is by making it a priority in their lives.

- **We must provide quality to the lives of our children!** We must be sure that we create an atmosphere of open discussion of critical issues with our children.

- **This is not a part-time job ... there is no such thing as "quality time."** There is *TIME*, period! To do a good job raising our children, we must give them our time—and lots of it!

Chapter 11

Turning Possibilities into Goals— Then into Actions

This is where we put that Top 20 list to work! As I have said numerous times in this book, to do a good job raising our children, we must give our time, and lots of it! This technique is also going to take lots of time. It's not something you can get through in a one-time sit-down. It must take place over the entire time your children are growing up.

The best way to treat a child is as if she already is responsible, capable, intelligent, and important enough to be given the tools of goal-setting. Teaching these skills says, "You are capable and responsible, so here are the tools to run your own life and make your own decisions."

As I said earlier, this is the farthest thing from permissiveness. You're not becoming permissive or allowing your kids to go wild and do anything that comes to mind. You will be giving your kids the tools for a *very* disciplined life based upon sound values they have selected. If you help them select good values to use in making their own decisions, the process of setting goals becomes an internal regulating mechanism that does not require you to be present. Goal-directed children are highly disciplined, guided by the only true kind of discipline: *self-discipline*.

When you give your children the gift of goal-setting, you give them a lasting and life-long tool to live fulfilled lives with maximum success and minimum disappointment.

Deciding What You Want

The first step is for your children to use their Top 20 list as a guide to setting their list of goals. Teach them to set short-term, daily, weekly, or monthly goals as well as annual and even life goals. The first step must always be to very carefully consider what goals they will select, because they'll be directing a great deal of effort toward their attainment. Getting practiced at that planning and consideration is also important, because goals are neither frozen nor finite: We are *always* adding and refining them.

At every opportunity, remind them that the ideas in their head will rule their world and that nobody else can put an idea in their head without their consent. By choosing the ideas they live by, they are in charge of the direction of their own life! (As I have already said, many parents consider religious teachings to be of great help in selecting the ideas that formulate their children's choices.)

Applying the "Three P's" of Goal-Setting

I will try to break down some universally accepted principals for wording and setting realistic goals by calling them the "Three P's" of goal-setting: Personal, Present, and Positive.

Personal

Help your children to divide the world into two parts: the part they can control, and the part they can't. Then have them focus their goals only on the part of the world they can control.

Often as I help kids set goals, they unknowingly set themselves up for failure by setting goals in areas they cannot control! I see kids setting goals to get straight A's in school or to be a starter on an athletic team. Both grades and starting lineups are controlled by someone else—the teacher or the coach. Help your children to word their goals to aim for things that are in their control.

If they want to achieve excellence in school, help them to write things like: "I always get to class on time. I complete every assignment and turn it in on time. I obey all classroom rules. I study for every class every night, even if I don't have a specific assignment. I always ask questions when I don't completely understand. I am always cheerful and respect my teachers even if I don't particularly like them." Point out to your children that students who do all of those things usually get pretty good grades. Then show them the bottom line: If they do these things, they have done their best and that is all they can do. Continually point out to them that the reward for giving their best is how good it makes them feel. When their rewards come from inside, their achievement of their goal is in their control!

This can also be an activity for kids who are anywhere between two and five. The goals simply have to be simple and structured. It might be worthwhile to help them set a goal to clean up their toys before dinner. Help them to see that it feels good to have things in their place before going to bed, and that it feels especially good to get up in the morning and have all their toys be easy to find. Help them to find reward in having a routine at the end of the day. They may need a lot of guidance, but building a picture of order and tidiness in the young child's mind ahead of the action will help them develop the habit of thinking through the plan before attacking a task. Sit down with them and discuss a simple plan for evening activities. Visualize for them what you will say, how they will respond, and how the toy shelves will look. Have them role-play this before the actual ritual begins. Then, as time goes on, have them take on bigger and bigger tasks and set bigger and bigger goals.

Give them an allowance and help them set a goal of buying a particular toy or game they want. Help them find out how much it costs and determine how much to set aside each week. Figure out how long it will take to save the money, then chart it on a calendar so your children can mark off the days and see the progress toward the goal. As you check the calendar together, discuss with them the lessons they are learning about discipline, patience, and fiscal responsibility. Many parents will give kids an allowance and then point out the mistakes the kids make managing their money. You'll be different. You'll teach your kid *how* to manage money. You might be surprised how little guidance and encouragement it takes to build the concept of goal-setting in your children's mind when the reward is that long-awaited game!

As your children get older, simply help them set bigger goals and help them to focus on things that they can control. Always work with them on goals they choose to share with you, and never ask them if it is one of their Top 20. Simply be available to help them to set some goals.

As kids get older, it usually works well to have some family goals that you all work on together. Set a goal to take a trip. Create the plan together—the destination, the cost, the length of time—and begin working toward the goal. Be sure to delegate tasks for each member of the family. If you are going to be camping, have someone get the camping gear in order. Have someone visit a travel agency to get brochures. Investigate online. In this way you will be actually setting a goal with your kids about a real activity and giving them practice in creating it and carrying it out.

As your kids get older, take on some bigger tasks and set some bigger goals. Some might be shared family goals like buying a big item, like a car or a big-screen TV. What a wonderful experience for kids to go through the process of budgeting and selecting a car to meet your family's needs! Don't be surprised if you watch your kids using similar tactics as they make decisions about their personal items.

Also, set some goals as a family for value-based actions. Set a family goal to say something positive about each member of the family each day. Set a goal to say, "Good morning! I'm glad to see you" each morning. Set a goal to find something funny to share with the family each day. Your goal can be really fun, and it may even make things better for you in the process! You might hear some funny jokes and be included in some great gags. My granddad always asked me to have a joke for him whenever I saw him. So I did! Every time they were coming for a visit or we were going there, I searched for a joke or funny story to tell him. In doing that, I learned a lifetime habit of finding funny stories and remembering them. He didn't propose it as a goal-setting activity, but he did teach me to have a plan of looking for funny stories.

When you have a plan to instruct your children about how to take their Top 20 list and word those items into goals, you will have equipped your kids with amazing tools of self-fulfillment.

I have often been asked, "If you could have taught only one lesson to every student in your class, what would that lesson have been?" The answer has always been an easy one for me. The one lesson I would have taught my students would have been, "Happiness is an attitude of choice; choose to be happy!" That one lesson would lead each of my students to a fulfilled life.

Present

Change is a "today activity." Teach your children to word their goals in present tense, as if they do, are, or have what they want right now—and then let them get started today. "I speak to my brother in a nice voice." "I cheerfully put away my toys when the timer goes off." "I carry my dishes to the counter after dinner." "I don't shout across the house; I go find Mommy so I can talk in a normal voice." So many well-intentioned goals never become a reality simply because the person never got started. Help your children set reasonable time frames for accomplishing their goals. If their goals are long-range in nature, help them select intermediate goals to measure progress. But above all, help them to start now!

You can do this by modeling the "start now" attitude with family goals. If your family begins to plan a trip, immediately write down the goal and start the process of planning. Write down "We are going to Disneyland in June" and put it on the refrigerator!

Positive

Effective goals must focus upon what you *do* want, not on what you don't want. Help your children to word their goals so that they state clearly exactly what they want. Just as I said that you must decide exactly what you want, so, too, must anyone who is setting a goal for his own performance. It really helps to word the goal with descriptive terms: "We cheerfully greet each other in the morning."

Writing family goals will help your children to write their own goals for things that they may not be sharing with you. Practiced behaviors are easier to duplicate. If you go through the process of wording goals as a family, it's much easier for your kids to set personal goals.

Watch Out for Roadblocks to Success

Many of the best-laid plans fail because of some common and well-identified roadblocks to success: the natural human tendency we come up against when we set goals. Failure to identify them and guard against them will often doom goal-setting behavior to failure. Teach your children to plan ahead and be ready to combat them.

In the following explanations I will repeatedly use the example of a young girl deciding to set a goal to get good grades in school. As you already have learned, the first step would be to change the wording of her goal. She should be guided to word the goal to only include things that she can control. When your daughter says that she wishes to get better grades in school, guide her to focus the goal on behavior that she can control by rewriting it to say, "I will complete all assignments, and I will turn in all assignments on time."

- **Pushback.** The natural human resistance to change. Help your kids see that any time they try to change, their mind and body will resist. They need to ignore the resistance, re-read their goal, and push *forward*.

  To demonstrate this to your kids, have them hold up a hand and then push on it with your hand. What they will do is push back, thus, the name. Let them see that any time someone pushes on them to change something about themselves, there will be a natural inclination to push back. It's the same when they set a goal. There will be a natural urge to resist that change so they need to be ready for it and move ahead anyway.

178

After setting the goal to turn in all assignments on time, if your daughter still is experiencing difficulty getting assignments completed and in on time, help her to see that this new behavior is a change for her. For a while it may be difficult to do work on time because this is a change from how she used to be. Help her to measure increments of success and to see her change in study habits as becoming the new norm for her behavior. Soon it will be difficult for her to not finish assignments on time because she will now have a habit of on time completion of assignments.

- **Rationalization.** Blaming failure on circumstances. It's only human to blame circumstances for any perceived lack of success. Parents must make kids aware that it is normal to do this, and that they must be aware of it and not let circumstances become excuses. (Talk about teaching accountability—this is exactly what you are doing!) Teach your children that if they have carefully written their goal, it will cover only what the individual can control. "If you encounter a setback, get out the goal, read it carefully, and try, try again."

The daughter who has set the goal to turn in assignments on time may begin to blame some circumstances. She may complain that she has no place to work. Help her to solve this problem rather than blame her difficulty on circumstances. Help her create a study place in her room, in an office, or in the family room. If she says she can't get her work done because she has a tough time remembering what she has to do, help her to create a day planner for remembering her assignments.

- **Projection.** Blaming failure on other people. Just like rationalization, projection is normal but very unproductive. Anytime we can blame someone else for our failure, we will. Kids must be taught that if they have written their goal correctly, then *nobody* can prevent them from achieving their goal.

The daughter who has set the goal to turn in assignments on time may begin to blame the teacher for unreasonable assignments or to blame a little brother for making too much noise and interrupting her attempts to complete her homework. As her parent, you can help by pointing out that this is a normal reaction to setting a goal of this nature. Point out to her that she has set the goal by working on the part of the process that she can control. If the teacher makes the assignment, you can complete it. If your brother makes noise, you can close the door, ask him to play in a different room, or you can move to another location.

- **Procrastination.** Putting off until tomorrow what you can accomplish today. Help your kids to use the wording of their goal to prevent procrastination by continually focusing on their timeframes for accomplishment. Help them to see that if they have measurable, short-term goals or steps toward long-term goals, they will be less apt to procrastinate.

  The daughter whose goal is to turn in assignments on time may experience difficulty getting started. Help her to overcome the natural tendency to put off new behaviors by helping her to establish timeframes and time commitments. Help her to select times to study that do not conflict with other activities she likes to do. If she likes to watch a certain television program on Thursday evenings, help her to create time in the afternoon to complete her assignments so she will be free in the evening. Help her to see that time is hers to use as she sees fit, rather than something to fight against.

- **Creative avoidance.** Dodging responsibility by simply not facing it. Help your kids to realize that their mind will help them forget to work on their goal by letting them become distracted by other things. Just like with the other roadblocks, referring daily to their carefully written goals is the most effective defense against creative avoidance.

  The daughter who has set the goal to turn in assignments on time may begin to avoid doing her work by letting other activities interrupt her. Help her to see how silly some of the interruptions can be. She can be distracted from doing a paper on the Holocaust, one of the most significant times in human history, by a rerun on TV. Help her to see what her mind is doing. Her mind is trying to get her to return to her bad habits by creating diversions. Teach her that once she overcomes just a few of these distractions, she will soon be one of those people who can concentrate on her studies in any situation.

This section is designed to guide you in helping your children to understand some common difficulties in setting goals and changing the level of their performance. Be patient and cheerful with your kids during this phase, because this is a time when your child is going to be uncomfortable. Try to establish a team relationship so your children see you as being on their side and not just a nag who is demanding unreasonable standards for their behavior.

Many parents find that if they concurrently set a goal for themselves and go through much of the same difficulties that their children are experiencing, they will find it easier to help their children. For example, a mother might try to organize her desk and the handling of the family mail as her daughter attempts to turn in assignments on time. Mother and daughter will really form a team to help each other see the pitfalls for each other. The daughter will probably learn as much from helping her mother as she will learn from actually doing her own homework.

If you really want to have a child learn something, find an opportunity for the child to teach the desired behavior to someone else. Besides, wouldn't it be a nice sidelight to teaching your daughter to get assignments in on time if you have a tidy desk and have the mail under control?

Chapter 12
Why Punishment Doesn't Work

Let me first say that I am not a zealot on a campaign to make the world a more gentle place by doing away with spanking and grounding children. My opposition to the use of punishment is simply that I don't believe it works to change human behavior!

If I thought punishment worked, I would advocate the use of it. But punishment simply does not *teach!* Granted, punishment can bring some behavior to a halt, but punishment does not teach the *desired* behavior. If a parent sends a child to his room for hitting his sister, I will grant you that the child is separated from his sibling and the hitting has ceased. But the mistake lies in thinking that future behavior will be changed by that technique.

Without instruction about what to do instead of the behavior that resulted in the punishment, kids rarely learn anything from punishment. Worse, they can learn the unhealthy lesson that the biggest person in the room gets to hit, or that it's acceptable to try to solve problems with physical violence and certainly with separation.

As a child I was sent to my room and/or spanked 5,000 times for teasing my sisters. I was told to go to my room and think about how I treated my sisters—and I did! I thought about what I would do as soon as I got out of my room: I would take them out behind the barn and hold their head under water in the horse trough until they learned not to tattle on me! (I was modeling what my parents were doing to me! They were punishing me for doing what they didn't want me to do, so I was thinking about how I could punish my sisters for doing what I didn't want them to do.) I was going to tie their braids in knots; I was going to stick gum in their hair; and I was going to throw their toy horses in the creek.

In addition to all kinds of mean ideas about my sisters, I began to form negative ideas about my parents. They weren't fair; I hated them, and I wanted to run away from home as soon as I got out of my room.

Now, if you've begun to believe that the ideas in peoples' heads rule their world, you can see that going to my room and being punished didn't create a single idea in my head that my parents would have chosen to rule my world!

It would have been so much more helpful if my parents had clearly defined what they wanted me to do and then (as I suggest in Rule 1) taught me how to *get along* with my sisters! If my parents had helped me formulate some ideas about the desired behavior for me to put in my head, it would have probably changed my behavior. But they resorted to the age-old and ineffective punishment method, assuming that it was teaching me something. It wasn't! I learned nothing about how to get along with my sisters while I was in my room.

Upon getting out of my room, I might have been a little more careful not to tease my sisters in the presence of my parents, but it did nothing to make me more effective at negotiating with them, interacting with them, compromising with them, or applying any of the skills that my parents could have taught me.

Getting along with members of the family is complicated, and it rarely comes naturally to children. It doesn't even come naturally to parents, as is evidenced by the degree to which parents lash out at their children during times of frustration. Parents often hold their kids to a higher standard of behavior than they hold for themselves. Many parents feel justified in hitting their children and shouting at them to try to correct their behavior but, of course, they would never allow their children to do so to each other, or back at the parent.

Figuring out how to get along with siblings while sitting alone in a room is even more difficult! Many other desired behaviors you want your kids to demonstrate will also be nonintuitive for them, and teaching the positive desired behavior is up to you, the parent! (Please refer back to Rules 1 through 5 for ways to communicate the desired behaviors to children.)

My parents might have come to me when I was making my sisters cry and suggested that I find a game where they used their dolls and I used some of my models and we collaboratively created a play using each of our own toys. They might have taught me how to negotiate with them so that the space in the playroom was theirs to use for an hour with their dolls and then at the end of the hour it became my area for my tractors and trucks. They also might have taught us how to share toys. I could have let them take their dolls for a ride on my trucks, and I could have used their dolls as drivers in my trucks. (Please don't go away from this thinking that our home was a battlefield between my two sisters and me—it wasn't! However, I do look back on that time and wish I had not made their lives quite as miserable as I did.)

If your kids are creating a disturbance at a fancy restaurant and you want them to behave in a more socially acceptable manner, punishment will rarely leave them knowing how to behave in a restaurant. I was at a restaurant the other day and watched a young mother and father confronted with exactly that problem. They had come into the restaurant and ordered a meal. Their kids began to act up even before the food arrived. The three kids looked to be about 7, 8, and 10. I watched as the threats of punishment escalated. Each of the kids was scolded, slapped, and made to change seats.

Finally, the father made good on his threat to make the kids go out and sit in the car. He grabbed the oldest by the arm and dragged him out to the car with the other two following. Once out to the car he gave each a spanking on the rear end and put them in the car. Then he returned to the restaurant, and he and his wife ate their dinner in humiliated, angry silence. They ate as fast as they could, wrapped the kids' dinners in doggy bags provided by the waitress, and left. On the way out, they apologized to the waitress and the manager.

In that whole scenario, I did not hear anyone offer one suggestion to the kids about how to behave in a restaurant. Restaurant behavior is not obvious to children! The punishment certainly did not teach them how to behave. It would have worked so much better for the parents to have practiced the desired restaurant behavior prior to getting to the restaurant. Waiting until the behavior had gotten out of line doomed any chances that the parents had of teaching.

Another common problem faced by parents is what's commonly called smart-mouthing or back-talking. A slap, a spanking, a loud angry scolding, or a time-out doesn't teach anything to a child about desired skills for communicating displeasure or disagreement. It seems to me that this punishment teaches kids that the way to handle disagreement is to slap, hit, separate, or get angry and shout.

A more reasonable approach would be to use Rule 1 and, at a time when both individuals are calm, the parent can simply explain to a daughter who has been back-talking that she will not listen to or react to loud, abusive, or angry expressions accompanied by nasty faces and body language. (That is the criticism.) Then she should end with a positive statement of expected behavior—tell her what *to do*. She might then describe the appropriate way for the daughter to express herself when she is displeased with something. She might tell the daughter to ask politely for the right to speak. Next, she might explain that all such statements should be made in a conversational tone with a pleasant facial expression. Finally, she might explain that the daughter should express her disagreement with—you guessed it—a positive statement of exactly what she expects, rather than a description of how mad she is or what is wrong!

It's always good to explain the rules of future interactions. The mother should tell the daughter that loud, abusive, or angry statements will simply be ignored. Nobody will argue back or even acknowledge those kinds of remarks. Next, she should tell her that all pleasant comments will be attentively listened to and considered. "You will not always get your way, but I will listen to your comments respectfully." It usually ensures that the message has been heard and understood if the parent asks the child to repeat this request back in detail.

Finally, the mother should follow the simple rule of honesty: "Say what you mean, mean what you say, then do what you say you are going to do." Mom must show the restraint necessary to absolutely and completely ignore inappropriate comments from the daughter. The mother should not respond in any way, especially not by reminding the daughter of the desired kind of response. Then the mother must wait for the daughter to respond in the manner prescribed. As soon as the daughter responds appropriately, the mom should stop everything she's doing and listen carefully to every word the daughter says. (This would be a good place to practice the listening words and phrases taught in Chapter 9.)

Does this give the daughter some help in choosing the kind of response that she chooses?

Positive statements about the behavior you desire will create ideas in your children's heads that will guide their behavior. Hopefully by this point you have learned enough methods for creating some helpful, constructive, and positive ideas for your children that this chapter won't leave you struggling for what to do! A simple way to practice your new teaching role is to try to eliminate "don't" from your instructions to your child. Instead say, "Next time I want you to …." Describe the child's body language, facial expression, tone of voice, and the words she'll use. So let's look at some of the reasons that punishment fails to teach.

A Definition of Punishment

First, I'm going to define punishment as any consequence artificially created by a parent as the result of the child's negative or undesirable behaviors. This would include spanking, grounding, sending to the bedroom, time-out, removal of privileges, withholding of allowance, standing in the corner, and so on. I am certainly aware these are the major tools parents have used for ages in attempting to control children's behavior. But that doesn't sway me from contending that these choices don't work!

Just because that's how you were raised doesn't make it right. So many people tell me, "When I was a kid, if I had done that, my dad would have ..." and then they describe some punishment ranging from spanking, hitting, or grounding to standing in the corner, eating soap, or writing sentences! Then they will say, "If my dad *hadn't* done that to me, I would *not have learned the lesson.*"

I contend that if the person learned the lesson, it was *in spite of* the punishment, not because of it. Most likely some other message accompanying the punishment resulted in the lesson being learned. Stopping using the "F" word because you get your mouth washed out with soap is different than stopping because you have been taught that it causes observers to judge you as a loser, because it is not acceptable in your family, because your little brothers will use it, because it is a sexual word. The key is that you, the parent, must teach the why and how of the desired behavior, not just stop the undesirable. I grant you that punishment might stop certain behaviors in the immediate present, but the mistake is thinking that the punishment has taught anything.

Accentuate the Positive

Punishment shifts the focus of both the "punisher" and "punishee" from the behavior in question. When a parent resorts to punishment, parent and child pay attention to the punishment, its fairness, and whether it has been enforced or followed. The child stops thinking about the *decision process* in his mind that brought about the negative behavior—and doesn't think at all about what he might do differently.

For years we have worked with prisons—those monuments to punishment remove the focus from positive behavior. It's rare that a person in prison focuses upon improved behavior without some guidance. Instead, he sits and stews about how terrible prisons are (and in most cases he's right) and how badly he is being treated.

When being punished, a child isn't engaged in creating thought processes that will bring about better outcomes next time. His fanny hurts, or he's mad about being grounded or sent to his room! The very act of punishing a child guarantees that reaction. Anger is a powerful emotion, and the minute the punishment is thrust into the mix, anger takes over the child's thoughts. In that state of anger, it is impossible for the child to focus on any positive thoughts. No attempt at teaching can reasonably begin until the child stops being angry and is calm enough to receive instruction about the desired behavior!

Punishment guarantees a pushback response. We're all human, and when we feel pushed or coerced, we push back. It's natural. You can observe it in your own everyday interactions. When a person crowds in front of you in line at the grocery store, it annoys you. When your boss tries to change a long-standing policy, you feel pushed and you resist it (if only in your head). A telemarketer interrupts your dinner to tell you of a wonderful new business opportunity, and you push back by hanging up!

Insert punishment into any situation and you get a pushback response. The pushback can manifest itself in many subtle but real ways. It may be very much like what you do when a policeman pulls you over for speeding. Your pushback can be subtle and involved. You're annoyed that the policeman stopped you, so you begin to find fault with him: "I don't like his manner," or "He doesn't have to be so pushy about it!" or "Man, he sure has an attitude!" Speeding may be unsafe, and maybe you shouldn't do it, but rarely do you ever respond to being pulled over by saying, "Gee, officer, I'm sure glad you pulled me over and straightened me out. Why don't you write me a big old ticket to teach me a lesson!"

Likewise, your kids aren't going to respond to your punishment by being receptive to instruction. Punishment focuses anger on the "punisher," giving children someone to be mad at. "I hate my mom and dad," is hardly the idea we want in our child's head, but that's the idea there in their heads as a result of the punishment we have meted out.

When they're mad, they don't have to consider—or, more important, *change*—their own behavior.

Punishment Doesn't Train or Teach!

Punishment-induced behavior "extinguishes" rapidly. Back when I was studying psychology in college, I took a lab course where we were to train a rat to do a task using some proven psychological methods. My lab partner and I trained a rat to do some simple tasks using two methods. First, we trained the rat to do the task in return for some small food rewards. It was a slow process, but it brought about a pretty high rate of performance. Then we trained another rat to do the identical task, but we used a small electric shock as punishment to shape his behavior.

I learned something in these little lab experiments that has stuck with me over the years and originally began my curiosity about the effectiveness of the use of punishment. The rat conditioned with positive reinforcement—food rewards—for his behavior always performed the task when put in the cage. Even months after receiving his last reward, the rat would perform his task at the same high rate. Without reward, his behavior would slowly disappear, but it would always return for a while when he was back in the training environment. Hope springs eternal, and he wanted that food! However, the rat that was "taught" by the use of punishment never once performed his "learned" task without being punished first.

Now, please don't jump to the conclusion that I've based a lifetime of work with children on a college experiment with rats! I simply bring it up because it began my curiosity about the effectiveness of punishment. Over the years, I've learned that if a behavior is "taught" using punishment, it will usually disappear the minute the punishment is removed! Also, if punishment is used to "remove" an inappropriate behavior, the behavior will return as soon as the punishment is not present.

On the highways of America, if there is no visible threat of a policeman or a ticket, how fast do people drive? How well does fear of lung cancer work to change the behavior of smokers? I've witnessed the same disregard for rules in children's behavior when the only reason to comply is to avoid punishment. If there wasn't a constant threat of loss of credit and expulsion, kids would seldom attend class on time. If kids ever find a loophole, they immediately take advantage of it! Behavior that has been shaped by punishment will revert soon after the punishment disappears simply because the child hasn't been taught to reason and find personal profitability in the desired behavior.

Punishment also traps the "punisher" into maintaining the punishment schedule. You made the rules, now you must enforce them. I taught for eight years with three typewritten pages of rules and consequences. Man, what a burden I created for myself! I couldn't even keep track of them myself, and I can guarantee that my students couldn't. I was constantly trying to correct every kid's behavior, and the kids would constantly accuse me of being unfair because I doled out a punishment to them but not to another kid for a similar offense. I couldn't keep up, and the kids wouldn't comply. I was really spinning my wheels.

Finally, I realized that I had much more success by simply getting kids to see the personal advantages of positive behavior. Having kids turn in assignments simply because it felt good to do so worked *much* better than threatening them with failure!

When we use punishment, we create a "me versus you" atmosphere. Remember that the ideas in your children's heads will rule their world, and it doesn't matter if the idea is right or wrong or even logical. When parents put themselves in control of kids' behavior, they almost always wind up being perceived as the bad guy. The goal *should* be to create an atmosphere in which kids comply with expected behavior because they *choose* to for personal reward and fulfillment rather that to comply with a bunch of rules just to avoid punishment!

Put Your Kids in Charge

I got to this point in a discussion of punishment while teaching a parenting class years ago, and a lady said, "I've had enough of this talk! I don't care what you say: My kid will never do the dishes without my threat of punishment!"

"Interesting," I replied. "So when your kids are 32 years old, will you have to go to their house and threaten punishment to get them to do their dishes?"

"Well, no," she replied, "when they move out they will do their own dishes!"

"Well, it seems pretty simple to me," I replied. "All you have to do is to create the same situation in your home that will exist when they move out. Why will they do their dishes when they move out?"

"Well, because nobody else will do the dishes for them."

"So create that situation in your home and free yourself of the insane schedule of punishment you have loaded yourself with. You built the punishment schedule, not your kids; and you are forcing yourself to hold to what you have created."

Still not getting it, she said, "So how do you propose I do that?"

"Simply this," I said. "All you have to do is to create a situation where your children *choose* to do the dishes. Here's how I might do it. Get each of your kids a set of their own dishes identified by color or pattern. Then tell them that when meals are served, they may only use their own dishes and silverware.

"It might go like this, 'Good morning, Billy, here's your breakfast. Sorry about the meatloaf on your plate, but it was left over from dinner.' And then later it might be, 'Well, Billy, here is your lunch. Sorry about the eggs and bacon grease, but that's what was left after breakfast.'"

Punishment doesn't teach accountability. Often when you introduce punishment, the kid turns it into a game of how much he can get away with without you catching him. The behavior you're trying to encourage becomes *your??* responsibility to enforce, rather than *their* responsibility to perform. If you take responsibility for your child's behavior at home, she will have to learn all over again to be accountable outside of your influence, and the outside world is a tough teacher! The goal ought to be to put the child in control—to make her responsible for her performance. Teach her the appropriate behavior and then let her be in control of it.

If you establish punishment as The Reason to Do What's Right, *you* have to be The Enforcer behind every action. If you have active kids, and more than one, the job can be overwhelming! Put your kids in charge. Let them experience the real consequences, rather than the ones that you create. If it isn't illegal, immoral, or life threatening, let your kids deal with the real consequences of their actions (or inactions). When we're adults on our own, the result of not doing dishes is ... dirty dishes. It's not being grounded or scolded or spanked. Why should it be different for kids? Teach them that they are *part* of the household—not servants trying simply to avoid punishment. If we want clean dishes, we have to share the job of getting them clean!

As I previously noted, a common problem for parents of young children is behavior in public places, like restaurants. Often what happens is that the parents spend the whole time trying to control the children's behavior with angry words, firm grips, and even slaps. Things degenerate into a very unpleasant and contentious situation—for the family *and* the people around them!

What could they do differently? A much better approach would be to practice the desired behavior at home. Practice the table manners. Practice the proper volume of speaking and the way everyone will speak to the restaurant staff. Thus, the standard of behavior is established and understood by everyone. Then go to the restaurant with the kids in control of their own behavior. Your preparation for the trip to the restaurant has established that the only involvement Mom and Dad will have in the kids' behavior will be to make the decision to leave if the behavior is out of line with what was practiced at home. The kids are responsible for their behavior and the parents offer only the final evaluation against the agreed upon family standard.

A discussion following the trip to the restaurant will really help to offer realistic positive reinforcement of the desired behavior. Statements like, "Wasn't that great, going to a nice restaurant and having a nice meal in a very pleasant atmosphere?" or "Wow, doesn't it feel good to go to a restaurant and know how to act?" The goal is to get your children to tune in to the self-motivating inner rewards for proper behavior. Get kids to make good decisions and find their own rewards for the desired behavior, and it becomes unnecessary for parents to punish them—or even be present—for kids to make good decisions.

The Right Way Is the Reward!

Most of all, punishment prevents children from experiencing the real consequence of their actions. The reward for good performance is good performance! Seldom is it necessary for us to provide the reward, and the same is true for punishment. The punishment for poor performance is poor performance!

If we simply point out the negative consequences resulting from negative behavior, we do not need to create our own. We can really help our children if we help them to foresee potential problems and natural consequences of their choices.

Sometimes, of course, we simply cannot let children face natural consequences. As we said before, if it is illegal, immoral, or life threatening, we must be the adult and step in.

It is not the duty of adults to create new punishments, but rather to point out the negative consequences inherent in the child's negative actions ... and most important, to suggest positive alternatives.

Taking Action

1. Identify a situation where you normally would have resorted to punishment as a tool to control your child's behavior.

2. Devise a strategy other than punishment that would help the child focus on the natural consequences of his actions. Refer back to the techniques discussed earlier in the book.

3. Help the child identify other behavior in that situation that would bring about a more rewarding outcome. Practice the new behavior.

4. Make note of the success of this alternative method of achieving the desired behavior without resorting to punishment.

Chapter 13

Dealing with Tragedy

A major question parents regularly ask us is, "How do we help our children deal with tragedy and disappointment?" This has been and will be a problem for every generation. Parents search for ideas to help them guide, reassure, and comfort their children through tragedies as large as September 11, 2001, as close to home as the loss of a parent or grandparent, and as small as the death of a goldfish or a favorite shovel left behind at the beach.

Dealing with tragedy is universal for all families. Tragedies are a part of life. This doesn't make tragedies any easier to handle, but it does acknowledge that we are all in the same boat.

The events of September 11 left all of us, in America and around the world, in shock. Like most Americans, I claim no special experience in tragedies of this magnitude, so I claim no "hotline to enlightened response" on behalf of kids. It is in a spirit of simply trying to help that I offer the following thoughts for parents during trying times like September 11.

Life presents grave circumstances to everyone, and kids cannot be excluded. We can never protect kids from the realities of life. Therefore, we must teach them how to handle the tragedies that confront them! Our actions, as adults, speak far louder than our words. As I said earlier, when my ancestors were crossing the plains in a covered wagon, I doubt very much that their kids felt safe all the time. On one tragic day, they buried one of their six children, and then made 12 more miles on their trip west. That must have been traumatic for the entire family, and I am sure those five kids learned much about dealing with tragedy and fear by simply watching their parents' actions.

Kids learn more from our back side than they do our front side! It is imperative that we, as parents, be ever mindful of what we do and say in the presence of kids. We must be ever mindful of hateful statements, even if they may be intended only as rhetorical comments on the situation at hand. We must be reasoned even when we're just thinking out loud, because kids often take what we say literally.

Kids are probably very well served by seeing that adults experience fear, anxiety, and times of great emotion. It then becomes acceptable for them to have similar feelings. It is even more important for them to see that these feelings, while deep, honest, and real, do not immobilize us. In this way, they will avoid being immobilized by their feelings.

There is a false statement ruling the world of some people, expressed with words like, "I simply can't deal with this," or "This is more than I can handle." The true statement we must model for kids is that everyone can and *does* deal with every situation facing them! However, the key is that we all get to *choose the response we use* to deal with what faces us! If a person chooses to lie on the floor kicking like a maniac and screaming like a fool, that person is dealing with whatever faced him/her. What we need to model for our kids in times of crisis and fear is that we can also choose to be calm, supportive, and thoughtful in our responses.

The first tool for helping kids during tragedy and crisis is to be in control of your own response. This does not mean that we show no emotion, but rather that in the face of terrible emotional and physical stress, we are still able to present a reasoned response. We can show our feelings while being mindful that as the parent we must be in control of our feelings. By being controlled and reasonable, we take the first step toward making kids feel safe in any situation.

We as parents must view these times of crisis as key opportunities for the expression of love to our children. To quote Chapter 9, "The time kids most need to hear that we love them may be the very time we feel least able to say it." During crises we can become so consumed by the event and our fear for the safety of our kids that we forget to confirm our love for them. We highly recommend that all parents remember in times of crisis like September 11 and its aftermath to go to our list of "10 Ways of Communicating Love to Children" and focus on two or three of these each day with each child.

Remember, the child who shows the most outside evidence of trauma is not necessarily the most in need of confirmation of our love. All kids need to know they are loved in times of crisis. Sometimes kids who are outwardly the most calm can be the most needful of support. Show them!

Hush Up and Listen

One of the key ways to express love is to *listen!* Give time to kids and listen carefully to their thoughts, fears, and questions. You may be shocked at the wisdom of their ideas and questions. Listen, listen, listen, and listen some more. This would be a good time to use the six "listening phrases" proposed in Chapter 9. Kids usually need time to phrase ideas and thoughts, especially when they are about large, consequential events. When listening to kids in times of crisis, it is imperative that parents be mindful not to fill every silence by immediately offering their own ideas. Listen and wait—give children time to express themselves.

Following the September 11 tragedies, news anchor Peter Jennings did an hour-long session with kids from New York in which, rather than asking questions, he simply asked them what was on their minds. The kids' comments were amazing. They were insightful, enlightening, and searching, probing into areas most adults would never have pursued, revealing what truly disturbed them. By simply seeking comments and listening to them, Mr. Jennings dodged the major mistake of assuming he knew the problems facing the children. I recommend you use a similar tactic with your children when they face tragedy.

The Precious Commodity: Time, Time, and More Time

During and after tragedy, give lots of time to your kids. Just seize the time available. Take a walk, play a game, do a puzzle, pick them up from school and go fishing or to the park, read a book, get down on the floor and play with blocks or dolls. Spend time with them!

For kids who are old enough, it will be helpful to spend time putting the events they are facing into historical perspective. Here is a great time for parents to draw on the wisdom gained from the experience of older generations. Seek out grandparents or other elderly relatives and friends who can offer accounts of their experiences in past crises, so kids can see hope for themselves in this new situation.

Times like this are an ideal opportunity for parents to guide kids in the selection of heroes and role models. As kids begin to make decisions about their own actions, knowing the personal stories of revered people who have acted reasonably and courageously in times past will help them find the courage to act wisely. Find books about people like Mother Teresa, Thomas Jefferson, Rosa Parks, and Martin Luther King Jr. Read together with your kids about these people who have shown great courage and leadership during times of crisis and tragedy.

Give kids historical perspective by drawing comparisons for them. For example, as you discuss the terrorists who perpetrated the attacks of September 11, it might be helpful for kids to hear questions like, "Does the United States have groups and organizations who have some radical, violent, and hateful ideas at the core of their philosophy? What about organizations like the Ku Klux Klan, the Nazi Party, the Black Panthers? Would it be reasonable to bomb the United States because of the actions and ideas of those small, radical groups? If those groups act upon their ideas of hatred and violence, what would be a reasonable manner of dealing with their actions?" Perhaps these questions will help you show your child that this tragedy was the result of the hate of a small number of radical people, and their violence was not a reasonable action. It happened because they were radical in their beliefs, but a violent overreaction might be equally terrible.

Democracy teaches self-worth. Democracy brings the great comfort that comes with having and using the ability to make decisions and exercising the right to take action. At times of crisis, as the parent and adult, it may be necessary to take unilateral and immediate action to provide for the safety of the family. However, as soon as possible, include kids in decisions about actions to be taken by the family. For example, kids might be included in selecting family activities like memorials to attend, prayers and meditations to be offered, ways to show respect and concern, news reports to watch or not watch, or ways and times to get back to business as usual in the home.

Expect Unexpected Behaviors

If your child reverts to a behavior he has outgrown, such as needing a comfort blanket, having potty accidents or tantrums, or wanting to sleep with you or in your room, it may simply be a cry for you to "notice me" or "comfort me" because of the stress of the event. As usual, try to ignore or minimize the inappropriate behavior and, as soon as possible, reward appropriate behavior with a hug or an invitation for a game, a walk, or some other favorite activity. If at all possible, avoid trying to teach or reason when the child is acting out. Simply ignore it, and when it ceases, use Rule 1 and tell your child what you do want. Use Rule 2 and be very careful not to attack the child with statements like, "That is so childish," or "You're acting like a baby." It will work much better if you say something like, "I know you're really upset over what has happened. Let's sit down and talk about the whole situation," or "Boy, it's really confusing when bad things happen. I'm really upset, too! How would you like to sit down and work on a puzzle with me to quiet our nerves?"

Times of stress magnify problems for both parent and child, and point out the importance of using solid parenting techniques and strategies. A solid plan is necessary for weathering difficult times. It is hard to involve yourself in your children's tough times if you have not been involved all along! During calm times, establish regular and enjoyable routines and activities so that in times of crisis you can revert to familiar territory.

There is a wonderful book called *When Bad Things Happen to Good People*. I highly recommend having a copy on hand as a resource before tragedy and disappointment strike your kids. I've purchased about 36 copies of the book myself—all of them "loaned" to students who were experiencing upsetting times in their lives. I have found the book to be very comforting to kids. I received my first copy from my mother when Carl Moore, a member of my football team in Benton City, Washington, died suddenly one day at practice. He was one of my favorite students, one of the most popular kids in school, and on the team. His death touched the entire community so deeply that it was difficult to pick up the pieces and move on. The book really helped me move forward, deal with my grief, and continue to teach and coach. I cannot recommend it highly enough.

The Four Stages of Grief

It might help to know that there is a widely accepted explanation of the four stages of grief. I will explain them briefly here, but I highly recommend you attend a course or read one of the many books dealing with grief to gain a better understanding of these four stages. *On Death and Dying* by Elisabeth Kübler-Ross is excellent.

Stage One: Denial

The first stage of grief is to attempt to deny that the tragedy is happening: "This cannot be happening!" "I don't believe this." Recalling your own feelings from September 11 will help you to understand what your children are going through when they confront tragedy.

I remember watching the television and thinking, "This must be some big mistake. Nothing like this can happen in the United States." I knew deep down that the events I was watching were real, but my mind was trying to deny them.

Stage Two: Anger

The second stage of grief usually involves getting angry, wanting to strike back: "This is so terrible that I want to find the person responsible and do something to them!"

Going back again to your own experience on September 11, I'm sure you can recall, just as I can, being so angry that you wanted to strike out at anyone who could have caused this terrible attack.

When tragedy strikes your kids, be on guard for their anger. They may strike out at something or someone without understanding why. Help them to recognize the feelings of anger for what they are and guide them to a healthy expression of their anger. Stop them from being hurtful or destructive; instead, guide them to some strenuous physical activity: tennis, running, a bike ride, or maybe climbing a hill near home. Have them write down their feelings.

Refrain from saying, "You shouldn't be angry." They are angry and naturally should be; it is a human response to crisis. Guide them toward reasonable expressions of anger.

Stage Three: Guilt

The third stage of grief usually involves guilt. "Oh, if only I had reached out to him, this wouldn't have happened." "What could I have done differently to prevent this from happening?" "Why do I still have a mommy and daddy when all those other children don't?" Guilt gives way to worry and fear about their own personal safety. It is natural for kids to worry about themselves. "If this happened in New York, could it happen here to me? What will I do?" This step is a personalizing of the tragedy. *When Bad Things Happen to Good People* is a great help here.

Comfort your children with stories of survivors or examples of wonderful things that can arise from tragedies. Andy Andrews, a comedian suitable for all ages, has written a series of books called *Storms of Perfection*. There are now four volumes to his great series. In his books, he explains how his father taught him to find the positive opportunities created in tragedies and difficulties. When I met Andy at the Children's Miracle Network national telethon, he told me, "I used to pray for an easy life, but after reading these letters, heck, I pray for problems—big ones!" He cites the inspirational life stories of hundreds of highly successful people who have overcome seemingly insurmountable odds to arrive at their successes. This book can be bedtime reading or family reading on trips to build a positive picture in your children's heads prior to encountering tragedy, and they're soothing reading as your child works through the stage of guilt or self-incrimination.

Stage Four: Acceptance

The final stage of grief is acceptance. "Well, this has happened, now what do I do? I can't change it." "I know I must move on." When the final stage of grief appears, the healing has begun. It is not finished just because the last stage arrives; all people will bounce back and forth through the stages. A child may accept the tragedy one day and then go clear back to denying it the next. For a week it may seem that acceptance has arrived for good, only to find that anger reappears. The only real danger arises when someone fixates in one stage and cannot move on. When that happens, formal counseling is generally in order. I will not attempt to deal with those kinds of extreme problems here, but knowledge of these stages can definitely help you watch for and encourage the healthy progression in your children.

I believe you know your kids better than anyone and are best qualified to help your children at these tough times. Explain these steps to your children as soon as you feel that they can understand them. I think that it is best to explain these stages of grief at a time when they are not grieving. During some calm time, it might work well to give them a list of the steps. It will help if they have some context in which to apply concepts like this: the death of a pet, the relocating of a best friend, moving to a new house, a fight with a playmate and subsequent loss of that friend if even for a few days.

The tragedy of September 11 makes a great example for communicating with kids because all of America experienced it. In discussing this event with your kids, you can show them that as a society we collectively went through the stages of grief.

Tragedy Can Build Commitment

One final thought that might overlay all of my comments is simple in nature but might be one of the most valuable to kids as they attempt to deal with this tragedy.

America is a wonderful land of freedom, respect, and joy. It remains so today, but it will not remain so without a total commitment from every citizen. The community we have in this great land did not happen by chance. It happened because of the hard work, sacrifice, and commitment of preceding generations, which have dealt with tragedies and overcome them.

Kids will not know what it takes to build and preserve our freedoms unless we teach them. Take them to meet everyday heroes in hospitals, firehouses, churches, care shelters, charitable organizations, and other places where they can come in contact with the people who make us a great society. Help them to understand what our flag stands for. It stands for the freedoms of expression, religion, speech, press, and all other freedoms we hold so dear. It might be even more important to show them that the American flag also stands for a nation that is built on service above self.

Freedom is not a birthright; it is earned by selfless service to community and others. Guide your children to find purpose for their lives in giving to their community through service to others. Help them to join their church, service organizations, and other wholesome activities as a way of building strong communities. Those involvements will really help out in times of crisis. Service to others exposes children to solutions to daily problems.

Guide kids into YMCA/YWCAs, Boy/Girl Scouts, 4-H, Boys/Girls Clubs, and other organizations whose mission is teaching kids to live lives of service. In doing so, we build a strong and resilient society for our kids to enjoy as we have, and ensure that each of our children personally knows that America is not defined by buildings and wealth but by our strong character and sense of mutual respect and support for each other. We are a nation built upon strong action by strong people overcoming tragedy and crisis. We are a nation of strong people, but it has been no accident!

Teach kids that freedom is only guaranteed by the efforts of individuals just like them, all across this great land, investing their own efforts in their own communities!

It seems interesting to note that many of the basic principles upon which this nation was created are the same principles that work for effective parenting.

God bless America and her kids!

Chapter 14

Expanding the Boundaries
of Your Home

Do not mistake the walls of your *house* as the boundaries of your *home*. It's a common mistake in parenting to think that it's possible to protect our children by simply making our own home a safe place. But we can make our homes totally devoid of danger and still lose control—because the actual boundaries of our children's "homes" include every place they regularly go in a given day, week, month, or year. The only way to truly protect our children is to teach them how to handle everything they encounter in their travels!

That may seem virtually impossible—after all, our kids come in contact with so much that we cannot predict or prepare them for everything. But the situation isn't hopeless. We parents can still have a strong, positive influence on our kids in their environment outside of our houses. There are many things we can do to create a safe and positive atmosphere in the community where our children grow and learn. Now don't worry, I am not advocating that parents become "Captains of the World" or the "Community Activists of the Century." What I *am* proposing is that parents can band together on behalf of their kids and work together to positively influence both the environment *and* the decisions that their children make within it!

The Concept

Here's the idea: It's a lot easier to teach simple behavior like table manners if every house your child visits has similar standards. If your child is eating dinner at a friend's house and sees his friend reminded to say "please" at the table, it might not be so hard to teach at home. Likewise, it is not so hard to teach children to set reasonable study hours if most of the kids they know have set similar study hours, and it may not be so difficult to teach concepts like respect if your kids' friends are being taught similar behavior. How do you create a community like that? It's really quite simple. Sit down with the parents of your children's friends and decide on some simple, common standards to teach and uphold in every home.

Believe me, this is not rocket science or brain surgery. As we travel around the country, we find that families are much more amazing for their similarities than their differences. We could hold a meeting and invite a Catholic family, a Mormon family, a Baptist family, a Presbyterian family, a Buddhist family, a Muslim family, an agnostic family, an atheist family, and two families who have no religious preference. Then we could have two blended families, a couple single moms, a single dad or two, and families from a few different ethnic backgrounds—and still, it wouldn't take long to find everyone agreeing upon some basic concepts we would all like to collectively teach our children.

We all want our kids to be honest, diligent, and hard working. Everyone wants his kids to put a high value on their education. Almost everyone wants his children to have a sense of their spiritual bearing, even though we might choose a different deity to worship. We all wish for our children to respect diversity. We would all like our kids to observe reasonable standards of health and personal hygiene. Almost all parents agree that use of mind-altering chemicals such as alcohol should be prevented in kids under the age of 21. Parents want their children to respect elderly family members. Almost unanimously, families want their children to be law-abiding citizens.

The point is that parents *can* come together and agree on the standards they will adhere to in the community in which their children will grow and learn. In most cases, they already agree!

Think about it. It would be infinitely easier to enforce study hours that become good habits if every friend that our child tries to call on a school night is studying and can't talk. It's much easier for our kids to have curfews if their friends do, too. It's much more possible to teach our kids to live drug-free lives if every other home teaches the same thing, and our kids learn the benefits of drug-free living from more people than just their own parents.

The same is true if your child is riding with the neighbors to soccer practice or a Girl Scout meeting, and the parent simply points out, "Hey kids, we're going to a really fun event, and I want all of you to notice that it is drug-free!"

Children do not know much other than what they experience. It truly does take a community to raise a child, and we need to purposefully build that community back into our culture. We must stop going to our individual homes and isolating ourselves from each other. We must talk and interact with each other—regularly.

So here is a plan! Start a Parenting with Dignity class among the parents of the children your kids play with and hang out with.

The "Plan"

To begin a Parenting with Dignity class, you will need some simple tools that are readily available. Almost all the information included in this book is also included in a videotaped (and soon to be DVD) format. You can get a copy of the curriculum by simply going to our website at www.parentingwithdignity.com and going to the ORDER page. If you do not have Internet access, go to the school or library in your neighborhood, or to your church, or to a friend's house where they can help you to order the tapes. You can also dial toll-free 1-800-811-7949 and order them directly.

Your set of tapes will come with the Parent's Workbook masters to copy for every member of your class. (The website has updated copies of the same workbook that are in a "printer friendly" format that you can use as well.) You will also receive a Facilitator's Tape, with many good ideas for forming a class and effectively involving other parents in building a community of support for raising your children.

The curriculum itself consists of nine one-hour tapes intended to be viewed one a week for nine weeks, with the time between classes spent by the parents in the class using the techniques in their own families. Each week when the class reconvenes, the discussion focuses upon the experiences parents have had in their own families.

Groups all across the country have used the Parenting with Dignity video curriculum in countless settings. Some hold classes in a school, a church, a community living dayroom, or in a juvenile court facility. Many people prefer the more intimate and friendly setting of a home. Many communities hold class each week in a different day-care facility, killing two birds with one stone by providing child care during the class and letting the day-care agencies display their programs to the parents. This also helps parents to be more informed about the options available for day-care in their community.

Building a class like this can serve as the catalyst for building a community to raise your children! Read on for many practical tips for effectively building a class in your neighborhood.

Effectively Conducting a Parenting with Dignity Class

First, remember this fact: *You do not have to be a parenting authority to conduct a class!* Our classes don't require "leaders" or "instructors." They're led by what we call "facilitators." Our experience all across the country has taught us that, without a doubt, the best facilitators for Parenting with Dignity classes are people who are *Not* viewed as experts or authorities!

Way too often, authorities and experts scare parents away. If you share our belief that discussions like the ones we are suggesting based upon this curriculum will create a positive community for your children to grow up in, then you, too, can become a facilitator! You need no special training. The curriculum is set up so that the videotapes conduct the class and the discussions are set up by the assignments that the parents work on in their own families. As a facilitator, you need only provide the location for the class and the television for showing the tapes. Beyond that, the facilitator is simply a member of the group.

A good facilitator usually answers questions with questions like, "I don't know, what do you think?" or "That's a great question. Can anyone use one of the principals from this course to come up with an answer?" Good facilitators share their own parenting frustrations and ask for help from the parents attending.

Getting the Families Involved

The basic steps to getting started aren't complicated. Here are some steps to follow that have proven effective in building meaningful parenting classes and create an ongoing forum for parents to create a positive community in which to raise their children.

The obvious people to get involved first are the parents of your children's playmates. If you can influence them, it will have a profound effect upon your own family. Just think how much more effective your parenting and guidance will be if your children see it practiced in all the homes they visit! All it takes is five or six families to begin your community's first highly successful and life-changing Parenting with Dignity class.

These become the *core families*. You invite those five or six families to an organizational meeting where you introduce the taped curriculum and give them your pitch on why this learning experience will be beneficial. When planning your pitch, think about the things you've learned in this chapter, and about things that are unique to you and your community: problems or concerns you may have that you'd like your core families to work to resolve, as well as strengths and common values that you've seen among the parents you've gathered that you'd like to see acted upon—and you think they'd like to see, too.

Share with them how much easier it would be for each of your families to teach desired behaviors if all homes had similar standards. Ask the parents you have invited to think about how all of you can create positive peer pressure in the circle of all of your kids by teaching them all some common decision-making skills. Share with them some parts of this book that have worked for you along with your personal experiences with your children. It generally helps to be a bit of a salesperson at this meeting, but if you're uncomfortable in the role of "selling" the mutual benefits of holding a class, you can just play the Facilitator's Tape for them. One way or another, you become the catalyst to lead this group to agree to meet and hold the class.

Then, together, you and your core families brainstorm and plan: locations, dates, meals, child care, and so on, so that the class schedule meets the needs of everyone as much as possible. (Food will generally increase everyone's enthusiasm. Have a potluck dinner or coffee and cookies!)

As an assignment for the first class, make each of your core families (including yours) responsible for inviting at least one "reluctant" or "at-risk" family. We all know one family where a parent has been laid off, a child is in trouble, a divorce is pending, or alcohol or drugs have created a problem. Even if we don't know any families in a true crisis, we all can name a family where the parents never attend a PTA meeting, an open house, or any of their children's activities or events. All across the country, people tell us that they don't know how to get those reluctant families involved. It may surprise you, but a face-to-face invitation from someone who knows them personally *really works!*

Getting Started!

What do you need to get started? It's really very simple. You need a room where all attendees can sit comfortably. As I said earlier, this can be a living room, a school classroom, a room at a church, a library, or a break or conference room at your job. Keep in mind that parents whose children are struggling at school may have negative feelings about a school setting. If you use a room at school, move the desks into circles, or push them together to form a tabletop so parents face one another.

You also will need a TV, a VCR, and copies of the handouts for each person attending. All handouts are in the Packet that comes with the tapes or are available in color from our website. These are the *only* absolutely necessary essentials. (Watch the Facilitator's Tape for some ideas for getting the copies of the Parent's Workbook copied off for free.)

Tips for Tearing Down Fences

It's important to recognize this common but mistaken idea in the heads of many parents: "Attending a parenting class is an admission that as a parent I have somehow failed or done something wrong." As facilitators we can know this isn't true, but if we don't address it head on, this idea can doom our efforts.

Because of this false assumption, parents will, consciously or unconsciously, put up psychological "fences" to keep out any information that might help them be better parents. You may hear, "We've tried everything," or "We're too busy," or "Man, you ought to see our schedule," or "What will we do with the kids while we're in class?" or "We don't have problems with our kids, it's the kids they play with who have problems, and we can't do anything about them."

To neutralize those psychological fences and false assumptions, you must plan carefully. What follows aren't necessary steps so much as suggestions to help ensure your success in building and conducting your class. If any of these sound like effective solutions to problems you may encounter, plan ahead and include this information on your initial advertising or invitations. Your core group will be of great assistance to you in this planning. The more people you involve in this process the better it will work.

At this meeting you might ask some of the following questions and be prepared with some suggested answers:

"How do we get the kids dinner on class nights?" Suggest going to your local fast food restaurants and asking them if they would be willing to support your efforts by supplying meals for one night of the nine-week class. Avoid using the word *donation*. Ask them to "partner with you" in making your community a better place for kids and families. You'll be amazed at the response you receive! Most of these companies are among the most civic- and charity-minded of all American corporations and will be glad to help—especially if you're asking for their product and not money.

Once you've enjoyed a burger dinner, a chicken dinner, a taco dinner, and a pizza dinner, go to the more formal restaurants and offer them a chance to compete with the fast-food restaurants by putting on a special dinner of their choosing. Many of these restaurants will be willing to host the banquet and awards ceremony at the conclusion of your course. Many will jump at the chance to show off the difference between their food and what is served by their fast-food competitors. In approaching these companies, be sure to point out that all the attendees at your class will be encouraged to frequent the stores supporting the classes with meals. Show the businesses that you can run the handouts from the packet with their logo on it for free advertising.

"What will we do with the kids while we are at class? We can't afford a baby-sitter or child care." You have lots of options here. First, go to the home and family life teacher at your local high school and see if extra credit might be possible for students who provide toddler care. Or go to local day-care providers and ask if they would be willing to bring some staff members over to provide care in trade for the opportunity to promote their operation. You will also be providing a real service to parents looking for a day care provider by letting them try out a few for free! As I said earlier, some people actually move their classes from facility to facility so that parents get to visit several during the course of the nine-week class.

"What do we do with our older kids?" Go to your local Boy Scouts, Girl Scouts, 4-H, FFA, YMCA, YWCA, and other youth activity leaders and offer them the privilege of coming to a class night and showcasing what they have to offer to the older kids of the parents in your class. Ask them to be prompt and to make their presentations fun and energetic. If you get with it here, you can have a really fun program each night of class, and the kids will be dragging their parents to class. Then set up VCRs and movies, music, games, art supplies, video games, or study areas as your space allows for the kids to use while their parents are attending class.

"How do we get dads involved?" The best way to get other men involved is to have one or two involved in the planning of the class! At least have a dad sign all mailings and have a dad listed as a co-facilitator. Each tape begins with a little 20- or 30-second clip of some football action—make sure the men see that. That's why it's there—to entice dads who might think it's okay to come to a class if it involves the NFL. Once you get them there, they'll keep coming back.

"We've run a class for 10 families—but we're just a drop in the bucket. How do we make this an ongoing program and eventually involve every family in the community?" Here is precisely what you do: In the first five or six weeks of class, your job as the facilitator is to select two families from the class to replace yourself in recruiting for and running the next class. (The people you will select will become obvious to you almost immediately. Generally they will be the most energetic and enthusiastic participants.) Then you court and train them to take over when you are finished. Give them the tapes, and promise that you will be available to help them duplicate the process. One class always produces two more and those two produce four and those four produce eight and so on .... *You don't have to do it all!*

Summing It Up

"It is better to light one candle than to sit and curse the darkness!"

As I have said before, too many people in this country talk about the younger generation as if they had nothing to do with them! We have an obligation to our children to teach them to live effectively in their world. We simply must parent them with dignity. We must be dignified in our approach and we must preserve their dignity as we teach them to be happy, productive, and fulfilled members of society. Being a parent is the noblest job on the face of the earth. Together we can build a better world for kids one family at a time.

Taking Action

Here are some workable suggestions for making the class you start—and any future classes—a success:

1. Involve your school to help motivate parents to attend class. See if you can convince teachers to give kids an extra 2 to 5 percent on their grades for having their parents attend class. Point out to the school administration that the school does not hesitate to deduct points for inappropriate behavior from the students, and you are just suggesting that the school give tangible rewards for parent involvement. You might get a couple of teachers or a principal to head up this effort.

2. Print tickets for every class you run and put a $10 or $20 price on them. It may seem silly, but charging money establishes value. If something is free, people subconsciously believe it has no value. We usually encourage people to set the price at $20. It works out to $2 per class session with a $2 registration fee. If your community is one where even $2 a week is too much for families to afford, then set the $10 price to represent a dollar for each class. Then if someone balks because of price, you can "scholarship" them, but when you give them the ticket, they're still receiving something of value. The money you raise can be used for beverages, food, or to support further classes. You can then take tickets to your local Department of

Social and Health Services or Welfare Office and give them some tickets to "scholarship" some of their caseload into your classes. Giving someone a $20 ticket to attend a valuable program is different than giving them a "free" ticket!

Believe me, the tickets really get people involved and keep them involved. People are generally suspicious of "free stuff" and charging a minimal price gives the feeling that this is a "grassroots program" built by the members of the community.

3. Talk to your local ministers association and seek the support of churches in your community for the classes. In many communities, the churches can be the most powerful advocates and advertisers for this kind of activity.

4. Speak to your local chamber of commerce. We have watched many facilitators garner huge support for Parenting with Dignity classes by getting the business community to support their efforts, from allowing employees to hold classes during the workday to allowing an hour off to attend classes. Some businesses will jump at the chance to help by offering needed meeting space or providing needed services like copying handouts or publicizing the classes in their businesses or newsletters.

5. Put up fliers announcing every class that you or your helpers put on. You may surprise yourself by finding a number of volunteer attendees showing up.

6. Speak to your many local service organizations, like Kiwanis, Rotary, Exchange Club, Lions Club, Veterans of Foreign Wars, and so on to see if they will help publicize the classes or help support them with donations for tapes and supplies. We have even seen some such organizations offer volunteers for child care.

7. Invite the local newspaper to have a family editor or reporter attend your class to do a special interest story about what you are doing. That will raise community awareness of what you are doing and help you to involve more parents.

8. Encourage grandparents to attend classes if they live in the community. The elderly members of our society are a huge resource that is often foolishly ignored. Many grandparents have a great influence on

their grandchildren, and it helps a ton to have them on your side. Having them in your classes will also bring a world of real life experience to the discussions. Remember, they have raised some pretty good kids—they raised you!

9. Enlist the support of the janitors, cooks, and secretaries at your school to help you put on your classes. They are some of the most powerful people in the community for influencing the lives of kids. Invite them to attend your classes. If they are involved, they can often get support that even the school administration cannot garner.

10. Enlist the support of the teachers in your kids' schools. You can invite them to attend the classes with you or you can organize a class specifically for teachers. It really helps to have teachers aware of what you are doing and supporting your efforts at school. They can reinforce many of the techniques you are using if they are on your team.

To get specific help with individual problems in setting up classes or to become connected to other families running classes in similar types of settings, just e-mail your question to Mac and Barbara Bledsoe (mac@drewbledsoe.com). When you come up with a great idea about something that has worked for you in creating a better class, e-mail us and we will share it with the world!

Appendix

Granddad Bledsoe's Sayings

My grandfather, Vice Admiral Albert McQueen (Mac) Bledsoe was a wonderful man who thought a great deal about values, morals, and ethics. He took very seriously his role of guiding his family to moral and ethical decision-making. He was one of the chief sources of guidance to me as I was growing up.

He wrote to all of us grandkids often, and often wrote sayings in the margins of cards and letters to us. When I would get letters from him, I would love to read the little bits of advice in the margins. At about age 10, I began to copy his sayings down so I could refer to them often and use them as the ideas to rule my world.

I offer these to you with the hope that you'll be able to use them in a couple wonderful ways as you raise your own children. First, I believe they make great starters for your discussions about values with your children as I advocate in Chapter 10. You could drop these bits of wisdom into the discussion over a family dinner and see where your children go with them. They will stimulate thought and discussion with your children on many important topics. Always ask your children to tell what the saying means to them in their own words. Ask them to offer their opinion about it. Establish that the only opinion you can't accept is, "I don't know!"

219

Second, I suggest you use these as topics for writing to your kids about your own beliefs and ideas. In Chapter 9, one of the ways I advocate that you communicate love to your children is to write to them. Simply write short essays about your thoughts on any of these topics. Offer them to your children as nothing more than that: "These are my thoughts on this issue and I wanted you to know what I think." Be certain to focus on the reasons why you believe as you do, so your kids can see how you came to your conclusions. You will be guiding your children in selecting ideas to rule their world, and using those same ideas for making decisions.

A third way that you might use these is for suggesting that some of the ideas might be worthy of inclusion on their list of possibilities for inclusion in their "Top 20 list." They might need to be reworded but might still be useful in clarifying some of those thought processes.

For lack of a better title, I call this section "Bledsoe's Wisdom." Of course, Granddad was never very careful about citing his sources—usually, he just wrote the saying and gave it to us—so I don't have many sources for these words of wisdom. It is not my intent to pass all or even any these off as my Granddaddy Mac's original writing. I simply offer them to you as they came to me. These were simply ideas that he wrote to me and to the rest of his grandchildren because he thought the ideas were worth knowing and using in our lives. If nothing else they make for some interesting reading and thinking, so share the gift that Granddad gave to me.

Bledsoe's Wisdom

A ship in a harbor is safe, but that is not what ships are built for.

We grow in the image of those we love.

A man is not as easily healed as he is hurt.

Be not forgetful to entertain strangers, for thereby some have met their best friends.

Knowledge in youth is wisdom in age.

"The greatest of all faults is to be conscious of none!"
—Carlyle

Preach not because you have to say something, but because you have something to say.

Those who never retract their opinions love themselves more than truth.

The best thing for being sad is to learn something.

Liars begin by imposing on others, and end by deceiving themselves.

Violent hatred sinks us below those we hate.

The opinion of the majority is not final proof of what is right!

If you can imagine it, you can become it.

If you can dream it, you can achieve it.

When you are at peace with yourself, any place is home.

If I never take my freedom for granted, it can never be taken away.

Pick battles big enough to matter, small enough to win.

The selfish heart deserves the pain it feels.

Do not pray for an easy life; pray to be a strong person.

Whether the glass strikes the stone or the stone strikes the glass, woe to the glass.

The teacher affects eternity; he can never tell where his influence stops.

If you cannot win, make the one ahead of you set records.

Kill time … and you kill opportunity.

Stop discrimination! Hate everybody. *(Granddaddy Mac was a man with a rich sense of humor and sometimes he offered sayings that were intended to provoke thought by getting you to laugh at the ludicrous nature of a statement.)*

A bigot has a concrete mind all set, mixed up, and hardened.

A lot of people who claim to have an open mind have a mouth to match.

No burden is too heavy when it is carried with love.

The mind, like a parachute, functions only when open.

Yawn! A closed mind like a closed room can become awfully stuffy.

Seize the day!

To a friend's house the road is never long.

"I believe everybody is ignorant ... only on different subjects."
—Will Rogers

If money grew on trees, lots of lazy bones wouldn't stretch to get it.

Spend less time shining up to the boss and more time polishing off work.

Don't look for faults as if they were buried treasure.

"To err is human ...," but when the eraser wears out before the pencil, you're overdoing it.

"Those who do not feel pain seldom think that it is felt."
—Samuel Johnson

A lot of people aren't afraid of work ... just look how they fight it.

A long life may not be good enough; but a good life is always long enough.

"You see things as they are and ask, 'Why?' I dream things that never were and ask 'Why not?'"
—John Kennedy

It is amazing what one can accomplish when one doesn't know what one can't do.

The biggest mistake you can make is to believe that you are working for someone else.

Isn't it a nice coincidence that you and I are both born during the same time?

Happiness is found along the way, not at the end of the road.

Happiness is not getting what you want, but wanting what you get.

To receive a present handsomely and in the right spirit, even when you have none to give in return, is to give one in return.

"No man is so foolish but he may not sometimes give another good counsel, and no man so wise that he may not easily err if he takes no other counsel than his own. He that is taught only by himself has a fool for a teacher."
—Ben Franklin
(It is interesting to me to see that many of the people whom Granddad took sayings from were people he either did not agree with politically or did not like. He seemed to think that he could learn from all people. He lived by many of his sayings. By watching him live by them, I learned that I, too, could learn from all people.)

A man is never astonished that he doesn't know what another does, but he is surprised at the gross ignorance of the other in not knowing what he does.

Group harmony is seldom achieved without personal sacrifice.

Success consists of getting up just one more time than you fall.

The probability of someone watching you is directly proportional to the stupidity of your actions.

When man is wrapped up in himself, he makes a pretty small package.

It is not what we have, but how much we enjoy what we have, that makes happiness.

It is not a wonder to see men as wicked, but is often a wonder to see them not ashamed.

Our wildest dreams sometimes result in our greatest endeavors.

Mother is the name of God in the lips and hearts of children.

Real problems can be overcome; it is only the imaginary ones that are unconquerable.

If a man does not receive guests at home, he will meet few hosts abroad.

You only live once! But if you live right, once is enough.

The way of this world is to praise dead saints and persecute live ones.

Absence diminishes little passions but increases great ones.

Beauty is all around those who choose to see it.

To understand your parents' love, you must raise children yourself.

If you want a friend, be a friend!

The only way to compel men to speak well of us is to do good.

It is better to remain silent and be thought a fool than to open your mouth and remove all doubt.

A man who keeps riches and shares them not, is like a donkey loaded with boxes of gold, eating thistles.

Quiet moments are life's rewards.

True love cannot be contained.

We cannot direct the wind but we can adjust the sail.

Two roads diverged in a wood, and I took the one less traveled, and that has made all the difference.

Four, five, six, seven, hate, nine, ten. Wouldn't it be wonderful if "hate" was only that number between seven and nine?

It is better to be a nobody who accomplishes something, than to be somebody who accomplishes nothing!

Keep your words nice and sweet. Someday you may have to eat them.

Ho hum, mediocre people are always at their best.

All things are possible, only believe.

I am not afraid of tomorrow, for I have seen yesterday and I love today.

Accept me as I am so I may learn what I can become.

I could help but I rather enjoy watching you do it.

Only those who will risk going too far can possibly find out how far they can go.

Find your limits and exceed them.

Dream and make your dreams come true.

Learn to bend instead of break.

Nothing is more difficult, and, therefore, more precious, than to be able to decide.

Have the courage to take off when others are sitting still.

You are never given a wish without the power to make it come true.

The farther you reach, the farther you will go.

Winter is the spring of genius.

The greatest pleasure in life is doing what people say you can't do.

All things are possible to him who believes.

The light shines warmest on those who reach for it.

The farther backward you can look, the further forward you are likely to see.

If you would have things come your way, go after them.

The greater the challenge; the greater the glory.

It takes courage to stand alone.

Give me hills to climb and strength for climbing.

Challenges are best met head on.

Live for today. Dream for tomorrow. Learn from yesterday.

Your world is as vast as your imagination.

Colors speak all languages.

I take the good with the bad and I shake it up.

Nothing improves my hearing better than praise.

The road to anywhere starts from where you are.

There's a paradise out there waiting for you.

It is easy to be critical. The real test is to come up with constructive alternatives.

It is hard to tell just one lie. The first lie so often leads to a second.

"He that cannot obey, cannot command."
—Ben Franklin

A group becomes a team when each member is sure enough of himself and his contribution to praise the skills of others.

When rejecting the ideas of another, make sure that you reject the idea and not the person.

If you will be patient in your moment of anger, you will escape one hundred days of sorrow.
—Chinese proverb

Like water, complacent people follow the easiest course. Downhill.

Children are the anchors that hold parents to life.

That which is bitter to endure may be sweet to remember.

Better to lose a jest than a friend.

A great artist can paint a great picture on a small canvas.

Harvest comes not every day but it comes every year.

The age of gold was the age when gold did not rule.

What he has in his hand is of no more use to the miser than what he has not.

A rolling stone gathers no moss!

A mother does not hear the music of dance when her children cry.

It is a worthier thing to deserve honor than to possess it.

It is the mind that enables, not the blood.

He who plots mischief for others prepares evil for himself.

It is no honor for an eagle to vanquish a dove.

If you wish to be loved, love first.

God grants liberty to those who love it.

Kindness is more binding than a loan.

Those who really thirst for knowledge always get it.

What the superior man seeks is in himself. What the small man seeks is in others.

Sorrows remembered sweetens present joy.

Necessity can make even the timid brave.

The problem with doing nothing is that you never know when you are through.

A book that is shut is but a block of wood.

He who loses his honesty has nothing left to lose.

To imagine is everything.

The righteous promise little and perform much; the wicked promise much and perform not even a little.

Gold is tried by fire; brave men by adversity.

There are two lasting gifts we can give our children—one is roots and the other is wings.

When a man does not know what harbor he is making for, no wind is the right wind.

If you do not understand my silence, you will not understand my words.

Kind words do not wear out the tongue.

Nature, time, and patience are three great physicians.

Better late than never! But ... best never late.

Everything has its beauty ... but not everyone sees it.

The law is for the protection of the weak more than the strong.

The smallest good deed is better than the greatest good intention.

Machinery has greatly increased the number of well-to-do idlers.

Magistrates are to obey as well as execute the law.

Talk not of wasted affection; affection is never wasted.

A man is rich in proportion to the number of things he can do without.

Music has charms to soothe the savage beast.

A single sunbeam is enough to drive away many shadows.

Nobody can make me feel inferior without my consent.
—Eleanor Roosevelt

Index

M-N

O

P-Q

T

U–V–W–X–Y–Z

"*Parenting with Dignity* is a must read for all parents. I am the father of three children and have been searching for years for good parenting advice. Unlike many other resources I have tried, this book gives you real answers and provides real solutions to everyday problems and challenges that all parents face. I am applying the concepts Mac discusses in his book and already am seeing positive results at home with my children. Thank you Mac Bledsoe."

—Joe P. Nolan, Coppell, Texas

"We have used Mac Bledsoe's philosophies in his book, *Parenting with Dignity* as a tool in our 'very strong-willed' granddaughter's life. She has made a complete turnaround and is an extremely happy and well-adjusted child … Thank you Mr. Bledsoe! It took less than a year!"

—Bob and Denise Morris, parents and grandparents Richland, Washington

"*Parenting With Dignity* will give any parent a renewed feeling of confidence. If there is anyone who knows about success in raising children, it's Mac Bledsoe. *Parenting with Dignity* is the most valuable book I have ever read. His 5 simple rules are full of lessons learned about guiding kids to make good decisions."

—Ric Huff, father, Salt Lake City

"I just purchased *Parenting with Dignity* for my sister and two cousins who are parents of toddlers. It now makes sense. Mac's son, Drew, demonstrates the utmost dignity in his very public career as a professional athlete. He is truly someone I admire on and off the field. Now that I have read this book I can see why he is such a class act. They say that children grow up to be complements to their parents. Mac and Barbara should be proud."

—Andrea Iacono, Reno, Nevada

"Excellent!! I came to work late today so I could see the *Parenting with Dignity* segment on the *Today Show* this morning. Can you please write me a tardy slip?? You guys looked great!! As Drew stated in his comments, teachers make excellent heroes and its nice to see you folks recognized as such. I am thankful I had the opportunity to sit in your classroom and participate on the field under your tutelage. Thanks for being a teacher!!"

—Dan Downard, former student from Benton City and now an employee relations manager

"My husband and I are very busy raising our four kids: Keith (12), Katherine (9), Karley (5), and Kenton (2). It is a lot of fun and a lot of work. I stay home with the kids full time. I have been so excited to get *Parenting with Dignity* and to continue learning all Mac's tips! I am just excited to have my old teacher's great book! Now I understand why I found his class to be such a respectful and dignified place!"

—Former student from Waterville High School

"Thanks Mac! Your book, *Parenting with Dignity,* is too late for my kids, but not too late for my grandkids! My 28-year-old son struggles with a crack addiction. My 30-year-old daughter has severe spending-impulse problems and is now possibly facing jail. I raised both of those kids on my own for seven years. Then I remarried and my new husband has really helped me. We now realize I cannot fix my kids *after* they are messed up. We needed to *start* with a plan. *Parenting with Dignity* is working wonders in the lives of our 4 grandchildren, who my husband and I are now raising. I sure wish that you had written your book 20 years ago."

—Mom from Oklahoma

"*Parenting With Dignity* is one of the best-written books I have ever read. You will be amazed at the parenting philosophies that will help you in raising your children … no matter whether you are just enhancing your own parenting skills or if you are at your wit's end from using different parenting techniques that do not work for your child. You will enjoy the personal details of Mac's life as you find they will relate to you and your own children. You won't want to put the book down until you have read through it once … then you will keep going back time and again for repetition! This world would be a better place if all of us parents read this book and acted on what we have learned!"

—Tina Tidd, mother from Wenatchee, Washington